How I Lost My Mind and Found Myself

Jim Stallings

*The names of the doctors and nursing staff involved with my treatment have been changed in order to protect their identities.

ISBN: 1-4392-6834-7
ISBN-13: 9781439268346

Contents

Very Old Friends

Everywhere Damian went he was watched. People watched him and expected him to slip up, to let go, to split away, and nothing made him angrier. With Damian, it was always time to talk about what he was feeling. He was expected to share with everyone.

He was different from everyone else ever since the day he was born. The way he felt and thought was always different. It was always hard for Damian to cry.

For the fact remained that Damian did feel. He felt more than anyone would ever know. He often sat at home surprised at the amount of feelings that rushed into his body, like a rush of early morning breeze. But nobody saw this side of Damian. He was only seen as different.

Paranoid schizophrenia. The words themselves frightened people. It reminded people of something to be feared, or something to be locked away in a basement, something dark and primitive. The light of society and modern medicine would call Damian sick, but he would call himself enlightened. His eyes were truly opened and nobody could see it. But Damian could see it, he could see through the masks people wear and could penetrate deep into the core of our very selves. He knew people, knew all about them from the moment he laid his dark brown eyes on them.

"I am no longer a slave to the little yellow ones." Damian whispered as he let the small bottle of pills fall from his hand. Modern medicine would call the little yellow pills a miracle in breakthrough to help s fight against the evils of psychotic disorders. What do they know, those who sit behind desks and white lab coats. He resented them, but did not hate them. Damian respected them for what they believed in, but he was no longer their puppet, their little white lab rat. He made the decision long ago that he would give up the little yellow miracles in order to live his life.

Having done this, he walked to the door and looked into the cold night of his front yard. The darkness crept over the entire backdrop of trees and the main road in front of his house. Damian loved it, every shadow, every beam of moonlight. He felt as though he were seeing for the first time, feeling for the first time. How could he resist going out into that dark, cold world? As he left the comfortable front hallway of his house and stepped into the night, Damian felt like a god. The feeling soon left him as he walked closer and closer to the downtown area. He knew he was meeting a very old friend, and that the meeting would not end well.

With every step, Damian inched closer and closer to Douglas. For months, people had been telling him that Douglas was someone to be feared and avoided, but Damian knew better. The pair had been through too many circumstances together. And after all, they were very old friends.

"Just point and squeeze; that's all you have to do." Douglas said calmly as the car sped forward across the dirt road.

"Are they still behind us? I don't see them!" Damian shouted. The sound echoed around the cramped space of the car's interior and came back and hit Damian in the face. He was surprised at the sound of the tone of horrible desperation in his own voice.

"Alright, now pull over and let's make this quick!" the older Douglas said to his passenger as the pair entered an area unlit by the streetlights. Damian's silver Mustang violently pulled over to the side of the road and stopped and was immediately blocked off by a second car, a white van. The van pulled up behind the Mustang as Damian and Douglas exited the car and drew their guns. Douglas wielded a fearsome Magnum revolver while Damian lifted the smaller weapon Douglas usually carried strapped to his ankle. The pair looked towards the white van, peered at each other one last time, and then Douglas pulled the trigger.

Click, click, click. The sound was music. It reminded Damian of church bells ringing on a cold Sunday morning. After three shots were fired out of Douglas's weapon, Damian decided he would compose his own dark symphony of clicks and bangs. The windshield of the white van cracked and the metal of its hood dented under the fearsome weight of the pair's bullets.

Douglas had to gently place his hand on Damian's shoulder to make him stop firing. In all the commotion, Damian seemed to have forgotten himself and he kept pulling the trigger. He felt so alive and full of power as he carefully aimed for the passenger's seat of the white van.

The pair stood looking at one another for a moment. Damian was surprised to discover that his heart was not even racing in spite of what had just happened.

"Get back in the car, you drive." Douglas broke the silence. He took the small pistol from Damian's hand and walked slowly back to the car. Damian listened as Douglas's shoes scraped the small rocks and dirt of the road, listened to the car door open and close. Damian soon followed and the pair drove off again into the night.

Something moved. Damian heard something as he walked slowly towards the downtown area. He stopped dead in his tracks and expected the worst, but it was only a possum creeping along the side of the road in the shadows. Focusing now on the present, Damian walked on towards Douglas, towards the place where they agreed to meet.

He was continuously looking over his shoulders behind him. Something about the shadows that lurked and danced all around him made him uneasy. He could see a car off in the distance. The sight of the two bright headlights reminded him of the past, of the white van, and Damian left the side of the road and crouched behind the trunk of a nearby tree until the potential danger had passed. After the tail lights of the car were far off in the distance, he continued his journey.

Bach's cello suite came to him then. It seemed as though the music shot up from an underground spring at that very moment to keep him company. Damian felt a rush of joy at the sound and he began to conduct it with his arms and hands.

How could he be sick? Doctors and others had called his mind broken and shattered, but his mind was a gift. He heard the music now as clearly as the sun shone in the sky, and people would call him sick. It seemed incredible to Damian that people could say such things about him. And at that moment, the music of Bach's cello suite brought to light a memory from his past.

"I'll be back later tonight. I need you to do something for me, something very important." Douglas said as he opened the door of his black Cadillac. Damian watched and said nothing from the steps of his front porch where he was standing. He watched as his old friend drove out of the end of the driveway and into the main road in front of his house.

Damian wondered about the nature of Douglas. He knew he had once worked for the United States Government from what Douglas had told him over a cup of coffee during their first meeting. He had apparently split away from his organization and had gone into hiding from them. Douglas was always on the move, always looking over his shoulder, fearing something or someone from his past.

Low frequency emitters. That had been Douglas's project. He told Damian at their first meeting in a diner that he had worked for an agency that installed what he called low frequency emitters into trees and telephone poles in order to control people's emotions and thought processes. They were designed to make people less violent, less capable of committing violent crimes. Perhaps tonight's meeting was about this.

Damian stood on the front porch steps for a long time before he went back inside. He heard the sound of rain on the window of his bedroom. He sat and listened to music, Mozart, Beethoven, and Bach in order to pass the time. During those days, before his mind was slowed down by the little yellow pills, Damian would speak and whisper to himself out loud in order to organize his thoughts, something that frightened people. Damian could never figure it out, why it was so frightening to people when he would speak to himself, or answer his thoughts, or answer those who spoke to him secretly, those only Damian could hear. But it did frighten people, it frightened everyone except for Douglas.

His cell phone rang. Damian answered. He was given simple instructions as to what to do next, and he followed them out precisely. He was to meet Douglas in his driveway in ten minutes. It was then about eleven o'clock at night, and the darkness and the shadows were all around the house. A light fog was dancing about the street lights across the main road due to the day's earlier rain. Damian retrieved the kitchen knife as he was instructed to do and he waited by the garage door. The edge of the knife gleamed in the dim light off the corner of the house as Douglas walked up the driveway alone. He shook Damian's hand and led him to the backyard without saying more than two words. He pointed to a small tree in Damian's backyard and instructed him to cut it down with the long, cruel knife he held in his sweating hand.

And Damian walked on down the main road, still conducting his secret symphony. He was nearly in the downtown area and was very close to his destination. Very close to Douglas.

He could see the small diner's "Open 24 Hours" sign off in the distance and across the road. As Damian approached the diner, he crossed the road in the darkest part, still fearful of the passing cars, although there were very few at that time of night. He entered the little diner and met eye to eye with Douglas.

Douglas was sitting there, wearing that same old black suit with the same dark necktie. His cold cobalt blue eyes met with the dark brown eyes of Damian and the two old friends smiled at each other for some time. Damian crossed the diner and took his seat across from Douglas. A waitress who spoke with a Greek accent approached.

"Can I get you something?" was the question she asked as she stared Damian in the face. Damian ordered a cup of coffee with cream and sugar and was wondering why she had not asked Douglas what he wanted.

"It's been there too long, you know." Douglas said as he leaned back in the booth and folded his hands on top of the table. Damian did not respond. "It's affecting your family and even you. Why haven't you gotten rid of it yet?" he said in a pleading tone of voice. His whole countenance took on a look of concern.

"Douglas, if I do what you're asking me to do, if I cut down this emitter, do you think anyone will understand? No. All it's going to do is land me in some locked mental ward for a third time. I've already been where I don't belong and I don't want to be forced to go back there again when I don't even belong there in the first place!"

People in the neighboring booths began to turn their heads and eyes towards Damian. He was fully aware of all the eyes watching him. The waitress came by with his coffee with cream and sugar and placed the steaming cup in front of him with a strange look of questioning on her face. The Greek waitress looked as though she were very suspicious of Damian, and he did not like it.

The pair did not speak again for a long while. Damian finished his coffee and politely asked for another cup. The silence was finally broken by Douglas.

"It can't stay there. You know that. So what if you have to spend another week in the hospital, think of your family." Damian thought on the subject. He did not belong in a mental hospital. He only went the last two times for his family's sake. He just wanted to live his life and the only thing that would happen is more little yellow pills, or some other little medicinal miracle in the fight against mental disease that he would be forced to take that would only cloud his thoughts and put a clamp on his mind. He did not want that, he did not need that.

Damian finished his second cup of coffee and Douglas told him that it was time to leave. They both got up and paid for the coffee, making sure to leave a nice tip for the Greek waitress on the little table. As they left the diner, Damian noticed that everyone at the front counter was staring at him. This made him uncomfortable and he quickly stole out into the parking lot immediately followed by Douglas. When the pair was standing in the parking lot, Douglas said he had walked to the diner as well and they decided to walk back to Damian's house together.

They talked about their past and their friendship in the darkness and the shadows along the side of the main road as they walked. They recalled the incident with the white van and the unmerciful pistols, and Douglas recalled how dangerous it was to allow the tree in Damian's backyard to house the low frequency emitter. The whole time Douglas was speaking of the emitter, Damian did not say a word, he only looked down towards the shadows beneath his feet as the pair inched their way towards the house.

They entered the house through the back door and were standing in the kitchen. Damian offered Douglas something to drink and Douglas asked kindly for a glass of water with ice. As Damian turned to hand the cup of water to him, he was met by the handle of a long, cruel looking butcher's knife. Douglas held out the knife towards him and did not say a word; he did not have to say a word.

"Ok." Was the only thing that came out of Damian's mouth. After hearing this, Douglas followed Damian out into the backyard, and the pair stopped in front of the small tree containing the low frequency emitter. Damian raised the knife above his head and struck the trunk of the tree with all his strength. Damian did not care about what would happen to him after the tree was discovered cut down, all he cared about was Douglas. After all, he and Douglas were very old friends.

Introduction

That short story is the result of the last time a psychiatrist asked me to keep a journal of my symptoms. I wrote it back in high school during my senior year, and I assure you that my feelings and my attitude about my unique situation have changed drastically since then. All the events in the short story are true, meaning that I did personally, although perhaps not physically, experience those incidents and the only thing that I changed about it is my name, which I changed to Damian. There is no real reason for the name change; I have just always liked the name Damian.

With this book, I hope to revolutionize the way in which the world views people who suffer from—or enjoy living with—mental illness, myself being included in the latter. I do not consider myself ill at all, and that is the central idea and reason that I have written this book. What I feel needs to change is the entire perception and the views the world has on this touchy subject, which many people are afraid or even embarrassed to talk about openly.

This book is a personal account of my life thus far, my experiences with schizophrenia, and the outlook, philosophies, and lessons I have learned because of it. During my personal experiences and research, I have found that there is an unchecked and widespread form of discrimination against people who have been diagnosed with some kind of mental illness. This discrimination is hard to fully understand and even harder to calculate because it most often occurs hand in hand with the fields of medicine, health care, and the legal and judicial systems that are in place, which for the most part exist in order to help people.

I hope that with this book, I will stem the discriminatory practices that are in place in the world and work to change the way people in general feel towards mental patients. I also realize that this goal is very ambitious and will take much more than what I alone can accomplish merely with this collection of paper and words. The changes I am talking about and sincerely hoping will occur are only going to come about when readers of this book, and others like it, honestly take the messages inside to heart.

I also would like to point out that I am in no way preaching that mental health workers, doctors, or the fields of psychiatry or psychology are wrong or detrimental. I am simply providing you the reader with a different way to look at and to understand people who have been diagnosed with some sort of mental illness or disorder.

The problem I see and can bear witness to is that mental illness is exactly that: mental. It happens exclusively within an individual person's brain, which is extremely difficult for other people to gain control of and even harder to understand for very obvious reasons. The human brain is capable of so many amazing things in its own self-contained little universe of endless possibility and imagination, but when its systems deteriorate or become skewed, it can make it extremely hard for a person to function, interact, be understood in society, and retain a job, and it can often ruin many people's lives.

The problems that arise with this situation are that no two people are alike. Every human brain is extremely unique to that person, and when large groups of people are put into the many mental illness categories that exist, it can be unnecessarily limiting. Some of us never get the chance to live our lives the way we want to, and it can take making a very risky decision and the strength to see it through until a person can be truly happy with who he or she is.

What I mean by categories and people being lumped into those categories is that when a person is diagnosed with a mental illness, that person's symptoms can be looked up in a medical book where the author has written about the many generalities that diagnosis exhibits and the treatment options that patient now faces. These treatment options almost always include some sort of medication(s) and a very long list of problems that the patient will face if he or she strays from their medication. These problems can be as serious as spending the rest of your life in and out of mental institutions or even suicide. This way of thinking tends to trap people into believing that there are no other options open to them, and I personally know that the idea of endless amounts of pills that will have to be taken for the rest of your life in order for you to be "normal" can create some feelings of resentment, sadness, and intense frustration.

My own personal story is much brighter than that, however. I have been lumped into a specific category following my diagnosis of paranoid schizophrenia, and I have tried and exhausted more than my fair share of the traditional treatment options, and I can now say that I have personally found a much better way for me to live and work to accomplish my dreams and life goals. And believe me, I am crazier than any patient my many doctors over the years have ever come across, meaning my symptoms are rather extreme, and I assure you that there can definitely be a better and more enjoyable way of life. It only takes a firm belief in the decisions you make and realizing the fact that you can succeed, despite what medical science and the statistics might happen to tell you.

This may sound odd, but I enjoy having paranoid schizophrenia very much, which can be very confusing to people, and I do understand why. The way I experience the world is quite different than the "normal" individual, but I am more than happy and willing to bring anyone who is curious about it into my head. I am the happiest and most content nut job you have ever met, and I am damn proud of it. I think it is time for people to hear from someone who has played on both sides of the field, someone who has taken enough antipsychotic medication in past years to kill a full-grown bull elephant thrice over, someone who hallucinates every day of his life and attended a Big Ten university and is able to retain a job, someone who has been happily off his medication for close to three years now and is in complete control of his life and has nowhere to go but up.

I sincerely hope my book enlightens you in some way, and I hope that you enjoy reading it and learning from it as much as I have enjoyed writing it and learning about myself.

Chapter 1
Background Information

Hi, my name is Jim, and I'm a schizophrenic. I have been living with schizophrenia for about five years now, and I enjoy it immensely every day of my life.

I was diagnosed with schizophrenia years ago back when I was a senior in high school, and it has always been my desire to bring people into my experiences and answer people's questions.

Although some of my family members and friends have told me that it might not be such a good idea to come forward and tell as many people as I have about my diagnosis and situation, I have never understood the reason why I should not. I have always been an open book, and to not tell the people close to me about this very eventful and important chapter of my life seems utterly ridiculous to me.

Jim Stallings

Since I made the decision to keep my open book mentality about my diagnosis, I have spoken to my high school psychology class, a panel of University of Michigan fourth-year medical students, essentially everyone who knows or spends time with me, four separate psychiatrists both in and out of the hospital, and one psychologist.

My own symptoms include hallucinations of all kinds, meaning that I hear things, smell things, feel things, and see things that are not there. This, I have found through my research, is quite rare amongst schizophrenics. Most people with schizophrenia who do hallucinate at all tend to only experience auditory hallucinations, mostly in the form of foreign voices, and many, many more are unable to form or think in coherent sentences, and some tend to sit in uncomfortable positions for hours on end.

I hear voices all the time. Not constantly, but essentially every day. In fact, it is hard for me to exactly pinpoint a day that has gone by when I have heard no voices at all ever since my symptoms have arisen. This may seem funny, but I feel kind of odd when I climb into bed at night and think back to the events of the day and realize that it has been entirely voice-free. It almost leaves me feeling like I forgot an important part of my daily routine, as if I forgot to take a shower or brush my teeth.

The voices I hear are men's voices, and I cannot recall ever hearing a woman's voice. There are usually two or three, sometimes as many as five or six, distinct male voices that speak amongst themselves about me, often narrating or discussing whatever I am doing at the time. They sometimes sound condescending, but that is rare these days, and they usually just point out and discuss my actions by saying things like the following:

"Oh, he's getting his laptop out. His dad gave him that laptop; it's much better than the last one he had."

"You're right about that; I like this one much better."

Basically, stuff like that is what they usually sound like. People, especially doctors, have asked me if I have any control over what they say, and the answer is no, I do not. I have often described it as like being involved in a discussion with a group of two or three different people where you never know and you never have any control over what the others are going to say or when they are going to say different things. All you can do is listen to them.

As far as the voices I hear go, I am not bothered by them, and I often answer and respond to them, sometimes carrying on lengthy conversations when I find myself bored and alone. I stress the word "alone," and I do this for other people's sake. I have found from personal experience that my sitting around and talking to inaudible voices tends to make other people uncomfortable, so I only engage in this sort of activity in private. However, I once spoke to the voices all the way across campus on my way to a class my freshman year just to see the look on people's faces, which I thought was hilarious.

I used to be frightened and confused by the voices before I had a better understanding as to what was going on in my mind, but now I truly do not mind them for the most part. Sometimes they can become annoying, for example like when I am trying to fall asleep or focus all of my attention on something and they will not stop chatting about this or that. Sometimes I use them to my advantage, and often they make me think harder about something, like the answer I am about to put down on a test or the next sentence I am about to write in a book.

I have also been interested in art for a very long time—ever since I was able to successfully hold a pencil, to be exact. In this day and age, an artist needs to have a fresh and original edge on his or her work in order to gain and control a specific new corner of the art world and thus become recognized and respected. I have many times in the past used my schizophrenia, more specifically the voices I hear, in order to create artwork.

I have used the technique I developed of drinking large amounts of caffeine, which I have found almost always, with the right amount, sets me into a psychotic episode. Then I wait until I hear voices, and I begin to paint while listening to their reactions to what I am putting onto a canvas and adjusting the painting to suit their likings. In this fashion, I have been able to produce a

5

Jim Stallings

great many pieces of artwork. Many doctors have not liked my approach to painting, as you can well imagine, but my point with all of this is that I now feel I have such a vast amount of control over myself when I am in the midst of a psychotic episode, and I feel that my having psychotic episodes can in fact be helpful to me, especially while I am creating pieces of art in my very own art genre, which I like to call Psychotic Impressionism.

I have found that my visual hallucinations are what interest most people though, and I certainly understand why. That sort of thing is so very far removed from the "normal" person's experience, and many people are very curious and have many questions they would like to have me answer for them. My most common visual hallucinations generally involve changes in the way things look to me from time to time. More specifically, colors will become very vibrant and surfaces will appear intensely shinier, people may take on darker or more pronounced skin tones or seem to have outlined features, and my eyes will become extremely sensitive to light.

6

How I Lost My Mind and Found Myself

I remember that one time back in high school I was at a homecoming dance, and visual hallucinations of this type began happening to me in a very intense way. The walls all around the dance floor looked like shimmering, rippling water to me, and the lights and colors of the different decorations on the tables and ceiling became intensely vibrant, almost to an unbearable point. It was like I had somehow transported back through time to San Francisco during the 1960s. Since that night, I have not had hallucinations of this sort ever become that intense; these days, I will begin to notice that the little cracks in sidewalks or desks will really jump out at me and catch my eye, or that colors, often accompanied by sounds, will become much more brilliant.

But that is not the extent of my visual hallucinations. If you recall the short story in the beginning of this book, I mention quite often and focus the events in the narration on a man named Douglas. Douglas is someone I apparently invented, and he is someone who exists specifically and exclusively in my own little world. There was a time—a long time, in fact—where I was

Jim Stallings

absolutely one hundred and fifty percent convinced that he was an actual walking, talking, breathing human being, and I did treat him as such, often in public.

People often ask me to describe what Douglas looks like, and a few of my doctors have wanted me to attempt to sketch him, but this has thus far proven to be impossible because any time that I have tried to quickly sketch Douglas, he left in a hurry, and I have never been skilled at drawing people's faces straight from memory, so I prefer to describe him in words.

Douglas is a tall man in his thirties, about thirty-five, with an advanced receding horseshoe-pattern hairline, and he stands at about six foot two or six foot three, as he is about an inch or two taller than I am. He has very distinct and vibrant cobalt blue eyes and a rather square face. Essentially every time I have ever seen Douglas, he has been wearing a black suit, and I seem to recall seeing him in or around a black Cadillac of an older model. However, remembering and concentrating on the details of our past rendezvous, I cannot be certain that the black Cadillac was his—meaning

8

How I Lost My Mind and Found Myself

I can't be sure if it was a hallucination of mine, or someone's actual car that I saw at the time of some past episode and for some reason attributed to Douglas.

Currently, Douglas does not come around me often, and I attribute this mostly to the fact that I usually ignore him when he does come around, which makes him quite angry. When he does come to me, he often appears behind me, shouts my name, and comes walking or jogging up in front of me to get my attention. When he does not run up to me in order to get my attention, he often simply enters the room or building that I am in and makes his way over to get close to me. I usually do not speak to him much or at all because he tends to show up when there are other people around, and in that case, I will pay him no attention whatsoever, and I will not verbally address him. This again is out of courtesy to others who might happen to find themselves around me.

The reason I do this is simply because he is usually being really annoying lately. He often tries to warn me of some danger that is coming my way, which I can easily recognize as not real these days. The dangers usually involve some United States government agency or the low-frequency emitters that were mentioned in my short story, and all I have to do is remember the experiences that I have had in the past and take much comfort in the fact that the other people around me do not respond to him or even give him the courtesy of looking at the strange man who had mysteriously entered my college apartment during a party.

All this being said, my hallucinations have been described by doctors as being very "impressive." I am somewhat of a rarity in the fact that I experience auditory, tactile, olfactory, and visual hallucinations, very often simultaneously. When Douglas shakes my hand, I feel a firm, rough human hand shaking mine, or when I hear voices speaking in my head, it is as though I am listening to people on a phone speaking directly into my ears. The only difference is that they are much clearer and do not sound electronic at all, and the voices speaking in my head are much more reliable than the phone service because I never get dropped voices, even in elevators.

Because my symptoms are considered quite extreme, when I was taking medications, I was taking a *lot* of medications. More specifically, I was taking the highest possible safe dosages that a person of my weight and height at the time could handle without risking an overdose.

Needless to say, I do not take any medications these days, besides ibuprofen for the occasional headache and my asthma inhalers. I stopped taking antipsychotic medications three years ago, and I have never looked back since. I have personally been on four separate antipsychotic medications in the past, one mood stabilizer, and a whole army of medications to help combat the side effects—and believe me, there are some terrible side effects associated with these drugs. For me, to be "cured" of my schizophrenia is not something that I am interested in. In fact, a friend of mine once told me that he wished that he could invent a pill that I would only have to take one time and it would completely cure me

Jim Stallings

of my schizophrenia. I respectfully told that individual to go shove that pill straight up his ass.

I feel that I have an interesting and unique point of view to bring to the table because I have tried living on and off the many medications that I have been prescribed in the past, and I consider myself an expert in my own personal case of paranoid schizophrenia, which I am happy to share with you.

Chapter 2
Woke Up This Morning...

My first hallucinations and delusions were more confusing to me than frightening. I recall many times having strange and very intense feelings of being watched or listened to come over me at odd times, or hearing people whisper close to me only to turn and find myself alone. I also oftentimes felt as though people were staring at me when they were in fact not.

I did not know what to make of these occurrences at first, so I simply kept things to myself and told no one. But soon enough, the onset of these hallucinations began to become more intense, which soon led to many frightening episodes that left me completely baffled as to what was going on in my life in general.

Some of the things that happened to me during this time when my hallucinatory and delusional symptoms first began to emerge were random occurrences that I have not seen or heard since. One time, the walls of my bedroom began to drip with what looked like blood that came from the corners where the walls met the ceiling, and the whole time I was thinking to myself that this could not be happening, but I would look again and there it still was. I could tell that these occurrences were not just my eyes playing quick tricks on me.

Another time, I recall walking into my high school from the parking lot and seeing a solitary man standing for some unknown reason on the roof of the school above the side entrance. I stood there in the parking lot for a short time and looked at the man, but I could not see his face, which was shrouded by the large black coat that he was wearing, but I did notice that no one else paid him any attention whatsoever. Again, I kept everything to myself, not knowing what to think about it.

These seemingly random—although quite strange and often frightening—occurrences seemed harmless enough for the time being, so I did not make too much of a fuss about them. But soon things began to take a turn for the dangerous.

One night early in my junior year of high school, I remember quite clearly waking up to some sort of scratching and rustling noises that were coming from outside of my bedroom window sometime after midnight. I got out of my bed, threw some clothes on, and looked out of my window through a small gap I made in between two of the blinds, expecting to see a raccoon or possum. I remember seeing a small figure jump back from my window and scurry towards the chimney, and the sight of this absolutely terrified me, causing me to jump back in likewise fashion and stumble around in my room for a second or two. After I saw this, I ran to the bathroom next to my bedroom and quickly opened the window and climbed out. I cannot even pinpoint exactly what was going through my head or why I decided to do this; all I can say is that I did it.

I got out onto the roof of my house, which is not very steep in the area near my bedroom, and chased after some sort of small-framed figure as he or she—or it, for all I knew—ran down the length of the roof. Towards the end of the roof, I recall grabbing at this person in the almost complete darkness, losing my footing, and falling off of the roof and landing on my back about fifteen feet below. When I got up and regained some composure, the figure was gone and all I had accomplished was that I got the wind violently knocked out of me and I almost threw up.

After this incident, I was obviously upset with myself for making such stupid choices, but I was thankful that I did not get seriously injured, which was a very real possibility considering what I had done. These feelings did not last very long, however, and within the next couple of nights, I found myself feeling very frightened of some person or thing that was trying to break into my room at night through my window. I was so scared of this scenario that I began to hoard knives and other weapons, such as a heavy metal length of pole and a thick length of dowel, in strategic places around my bedroom, most of them within reach from my bed. It was around this time that I also began to hear voices on a very regular basis on top of everything else that was happening to me.

At first, the voices came in what seemed to me like distant whispers, as if I were overhearing someone whispering to someone else as I was passing by, but every time I would attempt to find whoever was having these secret conversations, I would always be alone. This all changed in a short period of time, and the voices became much clearer and began speaking to me by name and asking me how or what I was doing, among other things.

I would often answer the voices aloud, as I sometimes do today, but at that time I would answer mostly out of frustration, asking and demanding things of them such as, "Who are you? Why do you know my name? Where are you?" to which they would never seem to answer satisfactorily or explain or go into details about who they were or where they came from.

The voices in particular had my mind going in a million different directions. For a while, since I did not know what to make of them, I began to think that maybe they were some sort of alien beings who were for some reason trying to contact me, and I connected these thoughts to the small-framed figure I chased off of the roof of my house. This explanation seemed to make at least some sort of sense to me at the time. I also thought that maybe it was God or angels trying to speak to me and apparently annoy me during class for some reason. During that confusing part of my life, I had nothing but far-fetched possibilities and even more far-fetched explanations as to what the voices were.

I did not know how to make sense of anything that was happening to me, so I continued my silence. I sought out answers on the Internet or from psychology books or pamphlets, and the answers I found there made me even more silent. I admit, I at one time fell into the same trap that most people, I feel, experience when they are going through something like this. I did not want to be labeled as crazy or go to any mental hospital, and I certainly did not, *at that time*, want that stigma attached to my name. So I continued to not tell anyone what was really going on, and I did hide it well, at least well enough to keep the people around me in the dark about these occurrences that were happening to me more and more frequently.

I continued for quite some time, maybe three or four months, down this road into some strange world that I was creating for myself, and the hallucinations became more and more intense, which were coupled with the feelings of being watched, spied on, and the horrible feeling that someone or some group of people was trying to invade my home for reasons that were unknown to me. During this time, I was looking for some different answers than the ones I had previously found online or in pamphlets and psychology books. I got the answers I was looking for in the form of a phone call.

Douglas contacted me early in the fall of 2004 during the beginning of my junior year of high school. I remember my cell phone ringing, the caller ID read "unavailable," and an older-sounding man answered me after I said hello. He asked me if my name was Jim Stallings, I hesitatingly told him that it was, and he told me that his name was Douglas.

He explained me that he was concerned for me and my family's safety, and that he really wished that he could meet with me that night. He actually picked the place to meet, which was a parking garage in the middle of downtown Plymouth, Michigan, and was about a five-minute drive away from my house. He told me he that he wanted to meet me in a public place so that I would feel safer and so that I could trust him.

I cannot tell you exactly why I went and actually met up with him. I suppose my mind was not as used to these things as it is now, and therefore I was unable to fully recognize anything in the situation that seemed horribly out of the ordinary. What you have to realize is that basically everything else in my world did not make much sense to me at that time, so this was just another thing.

I remember that I waited for about ten minutes in this parking garage, which is surrounded by other buildings and shops, before Douglas approached me on foot. He walked up to me and extended his right hand, introduced himself to me as Douglas, and told me that he was glad that I came and that he hoped we could work well together, or something very close to that. Of course, I immediately asked him how he knew me, and I inquired as to exactly what the hell was going on. He then suggested that we walk to a small diner not far from there to speak further about his business. We reached the diner in a few minutes, found a seat in a booth in the very back, I ordered a cup of coffee, and he began the conversation.

He jumped right in and told me that he essentially needed my help. He told me that he had until recently worked for a branch of the United States government that was involved in the mass control of large amounts of people, mostly in urban and suburban areas. Douglas said that he had split from this secret and dangerous organization because of ethical reasons. He explained to me that these people were actively placing what he called "low-frequency emitters" into trees, telephone poles, or other very common things and that these emitters were designed to control people's be-

Jim Stallings

havior, making them less violent and able to commit violent crimes.

I know that this all sounds pretty over-the-top and crazy, and going back and reading over what I just wrote, I would have to agree. But at that time, it was very hard for me to believe anything else. It all seemed, to me at least, to make perfect sense. Why else would there be people on the roof outside my window at one or two in the morning? Why else would I be seeing strange men standing on the roof of my high school? Why else would I be hearing these strange, foreign voices in my head almost every day? And most convincing of all, why else would I personally be acting and feeling so differently than I had been only a few months ago?

The help he needed from me seemed simple enough. He now had split from this secret organization and was personally attempting to reconcile what he had previously done as a member of the group. He was going from place to place, locating the low-frequency emitters, and removing them. He told me that he had located many of them in close proximity to my house, one even in my own backyard, and that he needed my help in order to remove them all. The way to remove a low-frequency emitter, he informed me, was to physically cut down the tree that housed it.

This is about the time when I went completely off the deep end. I recall being responsible for cutting down probably about twenty or so fairly large sized trees in different areas around my home, including a few in my own backyard in between the neighboring properties. I would use different tools in order to cut these trees down, usually a saw, but sometimes a large kitchen knife. Still to this day, I am not entirely sure how I never once got arrested for any of this activity.

I did not, at first, think that my behavior was at all bizarre. If any thoughts entered my head concerning the strange things I was doing, I would always seem to immediately talk myself out of feeling that anything I was doing was harmful or completely insane. I honestly thought that I was doing all these things—cutting down trees, hoarding weapons of all sorts in my bedroom, and slowly and carefully isolating myself from my friends and family—for the greater good. I figured, in my own strange way, that I was protecting the people I cared for and loved.

I did not talk to many people during this time, although I did not completely isolate myself from everyone. I did not want to make people think anything was going on with me, so I attempted to keep all my activity a secret, a job I found out later that I did quite well. I figured that if the people who were constantly chasing Douglas saw me too often with any one of my friends or family members, they might very well use that person in order to get to me, which would in turn lead them to Douglas. And according to Douglas, these were very dangerous people who were a secret agency of the United States government, and they could therefore do whatever they pleased to whomever they pleased. I feared that I might be endangering those I loved with torture and possibly death, something I wanted to avoid at all costs.

This behavior could not last for very long without being noticed, as you can easily imagine. But I was not found out by my friends or family; I actually went to my parents and told them a little of what was going on with me.

I had been doing some research on my own, both online and reading articles and books, trying to figure out what, if anything, was wrong with me. I began to become a bit suspicious of Douglas and the voices, especially when the voices and the odd feelings of being watched or spied on did not go away even after I had removed many of the supposed low-frequency emitters in my area. Things began to not add up for me, and I am very thankful that my logic and reasoning won out in the end.

I approached both my parents late one night after an argument the three of us had just had. They told me that they had been concerned about my odd behavior recently, and I told them in turn that I had been hearing voices and seeing things that I suspected were not there. This obviously came as a great shock to them and caught them completely off guard, and I remember that they did not know how to respond at first.

Jim Stallings

I did not tell my parents everything, as I did not want to make them worry any more about me, but I did lead them to the caches of hidden weapons in my bedroom, and my mom took them all away and hid them. I remember at this point feeling like an absolute lunatic, and I was certain that my parents saw me as one too.

But they did not see me as a lunatic. They told me that they were there to help me in any way that they could, and for that I am very thankful. My dad had seen a psychiatrist in the past following his double bypass heart surgery—after which he had become depressed, which is a very common occurrence following a major surgery and recovery like he went through—and he suggested that I talk to a professional about what was happening. I agreed to this course of action and tried my hardest to kick my shame to the curb.

But as it turns out, just making an appointment with a psychiatrist or other mental health professional is not as easy as it sounds. Everyone my parents called was backed up with patients for months, or did not handle the specific symptoms I reported to my parents, or did not accept our health insurance, or any number of different reasons they would not see me. The only option, it seemed, was for me to go to the nearest hospital and check myself in as an inpatient in the psychiatric ward, which was a course of action that was suggested by almost all of the private practices my parents contacted.

After about two weeks or so of trying to find someone for me to speak to, my parents and I cut our losses and drove to the University of Michigan Hospital in Ann Arbor, which is about twenty minutes west of our house. Once there, after about a three-hour wait after signing in, I first spoke to a social worker. I remember telling her that I was scared of what was happening to me and that I wanted any help the hospital could offer me. She wrote down my personal information and asked me to wait outside again.

After another two hours or so of waiting, I finally spoke to a resident psychiatrist. He asked me many questions about the symptoms I had reported to my parents and to the social worker and was greatly

Jim Stallings

concerned as to what was happening to me at that exact time. He wanted to know if I was hearing voices or seeing anything that I suspected was not there in the small room with us, and I told him that nothing appeared to be out of the ordinary. I remember thinking to myself that I was about to get jumped by three burly men in white scrubs and taken to a padded room at any given time.

After a short consultation with my parents and me, we all agreed that the best course of action and the fastest way I could receive treatment was that I should be admitted to the child and adolescent (I was seventeen at the time) psychiatric ward that night. So after a few meetings with social workers and doctors and many hours of waiting, at around two o'clock or so in the morning I was led over to the children's psychiatric ward personally by the nice young resident doctor.

Once at the unit where I was to stay, I hugged and kissed both my parents goodbye and goodnight and was then led through the locked doors into the psychiatric ward by one of the night nurses. The first thing I remember seeing was the colorful and extremely happy paintings of sea horses and dolphins all over the dull gray walls, and I remember thinking to myself that I was in the wrong place.

I was led by a nurse into a private room where I was asked many questions about my reported symptoms so that there could be a nice and readily available report for the doctor in the morning. I was asked to remember if I could when these symptoms began to emerge and what they were, and I answered all of the questions to the best of my ability. Throughout all of this, I could not help but feel like I was letting Douglas down somehow and that he may even find himself in some sort of serious, life-threatening trouble as a direct result of my actions. But despite all of these feelings, I continued to answer the questions the nurse asked me, and I filled out all of the forms she placed in front of me.

After a somewhat lengthy interview and a few questionnaires, I was led into another private room where I was asked to remove anything that I had in my pockets, and the few things I was carrying on me were placed in a box to be held until I was released from the unit. After that, a blood sample was taken to test and see if there were any drugs in my system (all the drug tests were negative). Then my entire body, *my entire body*, was inspected for any cuts or bruises before I was led into a room where, thankfully and finally, a bed awaited me. I remember that although I was extremely mentally and physically exhausted, I had the hardest time falling asleep that night; there was way too much to think about and way too much to process.

I think it was shock that I mostly felt that night. I remember lying there in bed thinking to myself, *I am in a locked psychiatric unit. Earlier today I was at home doing normal, everyday things. I have school tomorrow, but I obviously can't go because I'm here for God knows how long. What in the world is going to happen to me...?*

Chapter 3
The Good Patient

Thus began round one. I stayed in the hospital for exactly one week, and during that time I was put on an antipsychotic medication called risperidone (Risperdal), which is widely used to treat the symptoms of schizophrenia as well as bipolar disorder. I was also put on a regimen of many other medications to help combat the side effects of the risperidone, and I assure you that there were many.

This is also where I met my first psychiatrist, Dr. Thomas, who was working in a fellowship as a child and adolescent psychiatrist for the University of Michigan and regularly saw inpatients and outpatients alike. He was a very nice guy, a big sports fan, and he certainly did make me feel much better about my situation of being locked in a psychiatric ward. After a few meetings with him and the nurses assigned to treat me and look after me that day, the decision was made that I was going to be put on very, very high doses of risperidone, which I was going to have to take three times a day.

As I mentioned before, my symptoms are what mental health workers refer to as very "impressive." This means that because I experience auditory, visual, tactile, and olfactory hallucinations, often all at once, I was going to need the highest possible dosage of the risperidone for it to be in any way effective. This also meant that the side effects I was going to experience would be all the more intense.

Some of the side effects of risperidone that were listed on the piece of paper given to me about the drug the day I took my first dose included the following: fever; stiff muscles; confusion; sweating; fast or uneven heartbeats; restless muscle movements in the eyes, tongue, jaw, and neck; tremors; trouble swallowing; light-headedness; fainting; mild restlessness; drowsiness; blurred vision; headache; weight gain; urinary hesitancy; nausea; dry mouth; decreased sex drive; impotency; and problems obtaining orgasm.

How I Lost My Mind and Found Myself

The urinary hesitancy and the whole impotence thing I assure you was just a blast, and at one point or another, I experienced every single other side effect on that list, and some that were not even mentioned. Not only was I now an impotent high school student who could not even take a piss when he wanted to, but the risperidone also made it nearly impossible for me to think like I had previously been able to, which was by far my largest setback while I was on the drug.

This drug, and every other medication of its kind, affects everyone differently, but for me at least, it was like someone had put a clamp or a vise on my brain and all of its functions. It is weird and hard to describe to people, but I could not function the same way that I could before I began taking the risperidone. The normal little everyday things that I had to do—you know, like put clothes on in the morning or take the trash out on Tuesdays—had now become extremely hard or even impossible for me to figure out, let alone accomplish.

I remember that I would place the clothes that I wanted to wear to school the next day out on my dresser the night before so that I would not waste too much time in the morning trying to get dressed. I would wake up and look at my shirt, realize that it was a shirt, and then I would struggle to remember how to put it on and slip my arms and head through the sleeves for quite some time. It was the weirdest thing, but I honestly had an immense amount of trouble trying to accomplish simple actions such as that. I just could not for the life of me remember how to do even the regular, day-to-day things that I had been doing for my entire life up until that point.

This was obviously a problem for me because getting dressed in the morning and taking forty-five minutes to try and figure out exactly what actions were required of me in order to take the trash cans to the curb were by far *not* my largest concerns at that time in my life. I had to attend seven hours of high school five days a week, take tests and quizzes, and complete my homework on time, and it was very quickly coming to the time when I would be applying to colleges, which as many people know takes a great deal of time and focus.

But at that point in my life, I was willing to give the risperidone a try. I took my medications three times a day, and I spent most days with trembling hands, an extremely dry mouth, not able to focus or concentrate on anything, and generally acting like a zombie who resembled a mere shell of my former self. And to top it all off, the risperidone was not even making my hallucinations or uneasy feelings go away completely. It did make them less intense than before, but I was still hearing voices on a semi-regular basis, and I noticed that I was seeing Douglas a little less than before.

After I informed Dr. Thomas that the risperidone was not working entirely the way he and I had hoped as far as eliminating my psychotic symptoms, he suggested that I also begin a regimen of another medication called clozapine (Clozaril) in addition to the risperidone. Clozapine is an antipsychotic medication and is often given to mental patients in combination with other drugs that may not be eliminating their symptoms as desired. So after a few months on risperidone, clozapine was added to my daily regimen of medications, and the side effects grew even more severe. More and more medication was prescribed to combat the side effects. Some side effects of clozapine that were listed on the piece of paper Dr. Thomas gave me about the drug included the following: feeling short of breath, even at night or with mild exertion; swelling of the hands and feet; fever; weakness; sore throat; stiff muscles; confusion; sweating; fast or uneven heartbeats; sudden numbness or weakness, especially on one side of the body; sudden headache; problems with vision, speech, or balance; chest pain; sudden cough; wheezing; hyperventilation; pain or swelling in the legs; white patches or sores on the inside of the mouth or lips; nausea; vomiting; loss of appetite; jaundice; and seizures.

I have often gone to my friends and family members and asked them to describe for me what my behavior and general attitudes were when I was on all of this medication. They all essentially describe for me the same thing: they say that I was a zombie and that they did not even recognize me. My old personality had at that point left me almost completely. They tell me that I did not participate in conversations, did not even move quickly, and that I held an expression of staring at something far, far away with my mouth half open and my eyes glazed over for most of the day.

But even considering all of the issues that I was having with the side effects of the medications, I certainly did learn a lot during all of this, although remembering very specific things from this time in my life has proven difficult, which I attribute to all of the side effects that I was experiencing. I was going over to Ann Arbor to see Dr. Thomas about once a week following my release from the hospital to speak with him about any concerns that I had about taking the medications and to give him reports on my hallucinations and whether or not they had slackened or worsened. I told him the truth about my hallucinations and the fact that they were occurring slightly less than before, but I did not tell him very much about the side effects as I did not want him or anyone else to worry any more about me than they had been already.

Dr. Thomas also wanted me keep a journal of both my medication regimens and my hallucinations. He encouraged me to write down the time when I took each dose of risperidone and clozapine and to record next to it any side effects that I was experiencing three times a day. I remember all of the little things that my family did to make me feel better about what had recently happened to me. My dad even created an extremely sophisticated looking spreadsheet on his computer, and he printed it out for me to fill out three times a day; that still to this day makes me smile. Along with the medication spreadsheets, I kept a journal about any symptoms that I was experiencing, what day and time they were, what they were exactly, and how long the symptoms lasted.

As I mentioned, I did not report to Dr. Thomas about the intense side effects that I was experiencing because I wanted to conduct myself at our sessions as a model patient. I realize now that this sounds ridiculous considering how terrible it was for me to deal with all of the side effects that I just outlined, but I would ask you to try and put yourself in the position that I was in at that point in time of my life.

How I Lost My Mind and Found Myself

This was all very, very foreign to me, and I did not know exactly how to react to everything that was happening. A few short months earlier, I honestly believed that I was doing good for the people around me and thwarting some sort of government conspiracy by cutting down trees that housed low-frequency emitters inside of them, and now I was doped out of my mind on the antipsychotic medications that I was taking three times a day, having a one-on-one with a psychiatrist once a week, and going to multiple family group therapy sessions once every two weeks.

I learned a lot during this chapter in my life, however. I learned an enormous amount about the mental health professions and also about the cost of having something like paranoid schizophrenia. The total cost per month of all the medications that I was taking equaled out to about twelve hundred dollars, and the vast majority of this cost was not covered by my family's medical insurance, as it turns out.

Both of my parents told me that they were of course prepared to pay any amount as long as it was going to help me, and I was greatly comforted by those words and even more so by their actions, which always, always made me feel better. But I still could not shake the terrible feeling of lingering guilt. I was beginning to think that I was quickly becoming a burden to my family—both financially and physically—because I could no longer function the way I used to. I was basically no help around the house, and my condition made me not exactly safe behind the wheel of a car.

As you might have imagined, I could not stay on these medications forever. I took them religiously for about the last half of my junior year of high school and about one and a half months of the following summer. But after all that risperidone and clozapine, I decided to not take it anymore for what I feel are obvious reasons.

From what Dr. Thomas had told me, I realized that there were about seven different antipsychotic medications in the family and class that included risperidone and clozapine and that I could try different medications or combinations of those medications if the risperidone coupled with clozapine was not working, but I did not care. In my mind, I was done with all of that. However, I was not yet ready to handle life totally without medication, which I did not realize at that point in time. I developed that ability later on after gaining much wisdom and insight into my newfound way of thinking and experiencing the world.

I arrived at this decision on my own because I was basically too afraid to tell anyone, which was mostly because I did not want to generate any more worry and concern about me. Everyone around me knew about my zombie-like and unnatural condition, and they also knew the reason why I was like that, which was a direct result of my hospitalization. I also knew that many people were keeping an almost constant watch over my behavior. I also did not mention my decision to discontinue taking the risperidone and clozapine to Dr. Thomas for fear of him telling my parents or possibly having me hospitalized against my will; after all, I was not yet eighteen years old, and I was considered a possible danger to myself or other people.

Antipsychotic medications work slowly, as I quickly found out, and they take a long time to build up enough in a person's bloodstream before they become fully effective. The period of time that they take to successfully build up enough in a person's body can be as long as three weeks, depending on the medication, and it takes an equally long period of time to successfully leave a person's body.

So during the middle of the summer between my junior and senior years of high school, I secretly stopped taking the risperidone and clozapine and all the other medications I was on to combat the side effects. When it was time for me to take my medications, I would drink the water and hide the pills in my pockets to get rid of later when I was alone, and I would then make up some lie on the medication spreadsheets about my side effects at that time. As I expected, all the medicine was not out of my body until a little over two weeks, and then I was elated to be back to my old self once again.

I cannot describe in words how good I felt after all those months of being the zombie that I was; it was like I had just been released from death row. Just the little things—

like to be able to think clearly, play the saxophone again, and to be able to pee when and where I damn well pleased— were better than anything I could imagine. However, as you probably guessed by now, my psychotic symptoms returned as well, and this time they occurred more intensely and became much more real to me than they ever had before.

Chapter 4
Got Myself a Gun.

The next few months were by far the most dangerous times in my life thus far. As soon as all the risperidone and clozapine were effectively gone from my body, I began once again to hallucinate much more than I had before, and I also began to slowly not be able to recognize the boundaries between the elaborate fantasies I was creating and what was real. In a relatively short period of time, I was back full gear into that past frame of mind that the many mental health professionals who had known me, my family and friends, and even I to some degree, had worked so hard to control.

All the past delusions that I had fostered came back hand in hand with the hallucinations as well. I began to grow more jumpy, restless, and on edge, and I was slowly but surely accepting again that Douglas was an actual person with a very dangerous agenda. He told me that he was extremely glad that I had come back to my senses and stopped taking the medications that I was prescribed, and he informed me that he needed my help now more than ever.

These changes in the way that I thought and saw the world began slowly, but they soon picked up speed, and things began to snowball out of control from there. I was so wrapped up and consumed with that fact that I truly felt like my old self again that I failed to make the proper connections and realize that the things I was experiencing and the manner in which I was thinking was leading me down a bad road and closer and closer to one of the most disturbing and shocking events of my entire life.

Looking back on my decision to stop taking the risperidone and the clozapine during that vulnerable part of my life makes me question what I honestly thought would happen as a result of that decision. I know now that there were other options for me to exhaust long before making such a bold move, but back then I was desperate to return to my old self, no matter what the cost.

How I Lost My Mind and Found Myself

I did a very good job of hiding the fact that I was not taking my medications anymore from everyone close to me. I would even go so far as to act the part, to some extent, of the doped-out-of-his-senses mental patient who could not deal with all the little day-to-day things when I was around other people. Although I noted that most people noticed changes in my behavior and overall demeanor, I attributed this to their belief that I had finally become fully adjusted to the risperidone and clozapine, and I bolstered this notion by telling everyone that I was in general feeling better and more confident about my situation.

What I told to Dr. Thomas was the same story. I told him that I was still faithfully taking the risperidone and clozapine three times a day and that the side effects were in fact getting better and overall less and less intense. Dr. Thomas was always concerned about the side effects I was experiencing, most likely because of the high doses I was taking on a daily basis, and he was always worried that I might develop some sort of long-term condition from taking such high doses of medication. Whenever a person is taking medications of this type, there is most likely always some danger of a long-term adverse condition or lasting side effects, such as a Parkinson's-like inability to control muscle spasms that could potentially stay with a patient for the rest of his or her life, regardless of whether or not that person is taking the medication any longer. Luckily, this scenario does not apply to me.

I did not tell anyone the truth about quitting my medication mostly out of fear. I was very afraid that I would be hospitalized again—maybe even institutionalized for a lengthy period of time—and forced to take more risperidone, more clozapine, or some other antipsychotic medication, but I was most afraid of how people would worry about me. Trust was also another issue to me at this time in my life; I had a harder and harder time trusting anyone, and I found it easier to lie to people or to mislead them with deliberate actions in order to continue not taking my medications.

I also fell back into the belief that I was becoming a danger to my friends and family. I once again thought that they were in danger of being kidnapped and possibly tortured by the same secretive government agency which was responsible for the presence of the low-frequency emitters in order to get to me and in turn get to Douglas. I began to systematically and deliberately isolate myself from people during those summer months, blaming it on the side effects I was supposedly experiencing which made me not want to go out often with friends or my girlfriend at the time, who faithfully and patiently stood by me even though she knew about my hospitalization and mental condition. And slowly I became my old self again, but this time the boundaries as to what was real or fantasy for me began to deteriorate more than ever.

After only about four weeks of having no risperidone or clozapine in my bloodstream, I lost more restraint and behaved even more erratically than before my hospitalization. During this time, I would meet with Douglas nearly every night, usually by walking to meet him somewhere in close proximity to my house, or he would show up at my house at an agreed upon time, and during these meetings he would tell me where he had located more low-frequency emitters.

For the second time now, I do not know how I never got arrested for the activities I engaged in during these summer months as I was responsible for cutting down I estimate somewhere in the neighborhood of thirty to forty separate trees, mostly located in forests near my house and in the township-owned park that is about a ten-minute walk from where I live. I even ventured into the surrounding neighborhoods in the middle of the night in order to cut down a few of these trees.

I used a saw or a large knife to cut down these trees, which ranged from small saplings to larger ones that took about ten or fifteen minutes to successfully saw over. They would usually be in some remote and very dimly lit corner of a park or a neighborhood where they were not easily noticed. This, Douglas told me, was because the agency he used to work for would install the emitters at night and did not want to risk being seen by the people whose minds they were attempting to control. The trees would be located somewhat out of sight because that way, Douglas explained, they would not be regarded with any suspicion by the unknowing people who happened to live near them.

These activities became my main focus and main agenda during the midsummer months that I spent off the risperidone and clozapine. But soon enough, and after I had cut down a large number of trees, I would drive to different areas, guided by Douglas, in order to remove even more low-frequency emitters.

The reason I would engage in these nighttime activities—which I now regard as insane—was because Douglas and all of the feelings of being watched and the voices had all come back to me with such intensity that I believed them even more than I had before my stay in the psychiatric ward and the months of risperidone and clozapine that followed. I was not thinking clearly, and I was beginning to make some dangerous decisions that could have very well landed me in some sort of legal trouble or possibly even have gotten me hurt, but I believed at the time that what I was doing was right in some bizarre way that I cannot fully explain.

Like I had done before, I would begin to rationalize my behavior and force it to somehow make sense in my mind. Since all that risperidone and clozapine did not seem to work, I began to believe that I must not have needed it at all in the first place. Harboring thoughts like this made me all the more suspicious of Dr. Thomas and even of my parents, which I now cannot help but feel ashamed to admit. I remember that I even began to feel like they had gone so far as to have attempted to poison my mind by supporting and encouraging my taking of all the medications, which is a sentiment I have never felt since.

But eventually these thoughts began to give birth to even more self-fulfilling fantasies of mine. I began to believe that my hospital stay and all the medications I was on for the following months was all staged by whatever government agency was trying to control America's population, and I believed that they had done this to me in order to effectively shut me up. I would sit and think to myself, *This all makes sense now; no one is going to believe me even if I tell them what was actually going on because now everyone knows that I've been in a psych ward and have been taking antipsychotic medications for a number of months. Everyone's going to think I'm crazy and not take me seriously.*

I began to feel that all of it, the hospitalization and the medications, was staged in order to discredit me and sedate me so that I could no longer continue my work, which was cutting down and successfully removing all the low-frequency emitters that I could find.

The entire time I was engaged in these activities and coming up with these ridiculous revelations and ideas about persecution from the United States government, I was keeping it all a secret from the people close to me, and I found out later that I did a pretty good job of it, too. I was carrying out all of the tree-cutting missions late at night after sneaking out of my house or telling my parents that I was going out with my friends or my girlfriend, which was something they were never hesitant to let me do because as far as they saw, I did not go out or socialize with people very often.

As I grew more mistrustful of people and developed pretty far-reaching ideas about my own personal persecution—which is why I was diagnosed with *paranoid* schizophrenia later on—the more and more I would keep up the charade of being on my medication. I did not want anyone who might be part of this dangerous group of people who were attempting to halt my activities by hospitalizing me, which as far as I knew could be anyone, to know that I was back out destroying the low-frequency emitters they had so covertly been placing around the area. I actively attempted to keep a good poker face for the entire length of time that I was off of the medications, and I was paying extremely close attention to the words and tone of voice Dr. Thomas would use during our sessions and noting and dissecting my parents' exact words when asking me about my symptoms and medication. I did this to try and pick up on anything that I could use as evidence to prove that I was right and that some secretive group of people was trying to keep me quiet.

It did not take long for all of these feelings of ill will and distrust to result in a night during which a hallucinatory and delusional situation quickly and violently unfolded, a situation that I will never, ever forget as long as I am alive.

I do not remember the exact date of the night when this incident that I briefly described in my short story at the beginning of this book happened, but I remember everything else concerning it as clear as day. It was a summer night, a Friday, and school was not far from starting back up; I was going into my senior year of high school.

I remember that I had agreed to meet with Douglas that night sometime shortly after nine thirty so that we could be assured the sun had gone down completely. He told me that he would come to my house and meet me in the driveway that was in our front yard. I waited for him for about twenty minutes or so after nine thirty had come and gone. I remember feeling anxious at the thought that he might not be coming at all, which meant that he probably had run into some sort of problem, which you can imagine triggered my mind to run through all kinds of different horrible scenarios.

But I did not have to wait for him for much longer than twenty minutes. I heard someone or something moving quickly and noisily through the trees that flank either side of my front yard, and as I walked cautiously towards where this noise was being produced, I saw Douglas running very quickly towards me across the yard, and he looked absolutely terrified of something, like something was or had been chasing him.

Before I had a chance to ask him why he was so upset, he yelled at me, "Get in the car right now. We've got to get out of here!"

I had the keys to my older brother's silver Mustang on me at the time. My brother Mark and I shared this car for a while, and I drove it while he was a freshman at Purdue University in Indiana, where freshmen are not permitted to have a car on campus.

After Douglas yelled to me that we needed to leave in a hurry, we both ran towards the car, and I remotely unlocked it and climbed hastily into the driver's seat and started the engine as fast as I could. Douglas then turned to me without even taking the time to secure his safety belt and shouted for me to drive and make a right-hand turn at the end of the driveway.

I sped off after completing the turn and was driving and shifting through the gears very quickly, and I remember seeing Douglas whirling his entire body around so that he could look frantically and frequently out of the back window. I finally had a chance now to catch my breath, and I asked with an obviously worried tone as to what we were doing driving nearly sixty miles per hour in a forty-five mile per hour speed limit zone at ten o'clock at night, and I also asked him to explain what he was looking for out of the back window.

He told me that he had been followed to my house and that he had only noticed it right before he came running across the yard towards me.

I asked him, "Were they on foot right behind you?" as I was very concerned that there were now dangerous people in my yard and possibly in my house where my family was getting ready to go to bed.

He answered, "No, it was a white van."

After driving around for a little while, Douglas told me to turn into a neighborhood that was about a ten-minute drive away from my house in order to try and stay as much off of the main roads as we could as we made our way back to my driveway. I made the turn, and we went roughly in the direction we needed to go in order to make it back to my home. Along the way we made random turns, and in this fashion, we snaked our way through various subdivisions for about another fifteen minutes.

Douglas and I thought that we would lose the white van by making all of these random turns and thus putting distance between us and where Douglas had last seen it, but we were wrong. The van was waiting for us to return, hiding with its lights off in an entrance to a neighborhood that stretched for a few miles behind my house.

Before I knew what was happening, a white van just like Douglas had described to me pulled violently out of the entrance to the subdivision the second after we passed it. The van began accelerating very quickly until it was nearly touching my rear bumper, and Douglas yelled for me to go faster. I did not need any further encouragement, and I immediately downshifted and sped up to try and lose the white van again.

After making some random turns here and there for a few minutes at high speeds, Douglas shouted to me and told me to pull the car off to the side of the road up ahead on the left. We approached, still at high speeds, a very dimly lit road that was not very close to any houses or neighborhoods, and as soon as we got to a place on which the seemingly randomly erected streetlights did not shine, Douglas told me to pull the car over.

As soon as the Mustang came to a stop, I put the gearshift into neutral and yanked hard on the parking brake, not knowing what our next sequence of actions would be. While I was putting the car into park almost entirely from reflex and muscle memory without wasting a moment's time, I did not notice that Douglas had drawn both the enormous Magnum revolver he carried at his waist and that he had also removed the smaller pistol which he kept strapped around his ankle, which he proceeded to place in my right hand.

Douglas told me right before I pulled the car to the side of the vacant dirt road that all I had to do was "point and squeeze." I suddenly realized what he meant by that phrase, and I now understood exactly what he expected me to do with the gun he had suddenly placed in my hand.

The whole time after that I was running on pure animal instinct. The moral dilemma that I had at the thought of taking someone else's life previous to those last couple of moments I just described deteriorated the second I saw the white van pull up about ten feet behind us on that dark road. In my mind at that moment, it was time to make a decision I hope I never have to make again: Do I kill this person or be killed by him?

Needless to say as I have briefly outlined in my short story, I raised the gun, waited until I heard Douglas fire three times to see which of the two men in the van he was aiming for, and then I pulled the trigger nine times in the direction of the side passenger. The last three times I pulled the trigger were after the six chambers were emptied of bullets.

I watched the van and the outlines of the two men inside as they were being struck by the bullets that Douglas and I were firing at them from a very close range. After we both stopped firing, I watched as the two men inside stopped wriggling and writhing each time they were hit by a bullet. The whole event happened so fast that I barely had time to fully comprehend what had just taken place, and I was very surprised to feel that my heart was not beating out of my chest after everything went back to silence.

Many people will tell you very readily that they would never in a million years ever take the life of someone else. Until that night, I was one of those people, but luckily for me, the people whose lives Douglas and I took on that dark dirt road existed only in my head. But it took a *very* long time for me to fully realize that, and for quite some time I believed that Douglas and I had shot two people to death that night, people who were chasing both of us in order to do the same—we had just been quicker about it.

I had some very incredible feelings after the incident with the white van. It took me the rest of the night until I felt any pangs of anything other than excitement and adrenaline, but what you must understand is that the feelings of power and authority that I experienced immediately following the shooting are ones I would compare to a boxer knocking out another fighter when all of the odds are against him, but somehow it was very different at the same time. I felt a very strange mixture of power, feeling larger than life, feeling guilt, intense fear of retribution, and proud that I had protected myself from death. It is very hard for me to describe exactly in words what emotions ran through me that night, and needless to say, I did not sleep at all.

The next morning and day I spent as much time alone as I could because I felt that if I interacted much with my family, they would easily be able to tell that something was very, very wrong with me that day. I spent the afternoon watching news reports and checking local news stories on the Internet to see if anything was mentioned about someone finding two dead government agents in a white van anywhere near my house. I was not surprised, however, when I heard nothing about the incident in the news, which strangely enough only led to deepening my belief that the event had actually taken place. I thought to myself, *If these people are powerful and far-reaching enough to put low-frequency emitters into trees all over the country, they could certainly be powerful enough to clean up a van and make two dead bodies disappear without anyone ever knowing about it.*

I spent the next few weeks in absolute terror. I was still not taking my medications when the school year began, and the daily structure that school provided for me helped to bring me back down to earth a little bit. I still consciously attempted to make people believe that I was taking the risperidone and clozapine faithfully, and I did not tell Dr. Thomas that anything was out of the ordinary. To me, it seemed absolutely out of the question at the time to tell anyone—even my psychiatrist, who might have been a part of this whole conspiracy—about what had happened to me a few weeks before. I also believed that telling anyone about the incident involving Douglas and the white van could only lead to some very big and potentially life-threatening problems. The weeks I spent constantly in this mind-frame were a very intense and mentally draining time in my life as you can well imagine.

It did not take much time after the incident with the white van for my girlfriend at the time to realize that something was not right with me. She noticed that there were some big changes in my behavior and demeanor, and soon enough she began asking me questions about my medication, the side effects, and any symptoms I was experiencing. I repeatedly told her that everything was alright with me and that I was hearing the occasional voices, but other than that, things were under control.

She didn't buy it. One night on a Friday a few weeks into my senior year of high school, my girlfriend and I were in my hot tub, and she asked me to please tell her the truth about my taking the risperidone and the clozapine. I had felt as though I were ready to explode for weeks and weeks, and I felt that I was on the verge of a breakdown because I could not trust anyone and I could not tell anyone about any of the activities I had been engaged in for most of the summer. That night I told her that I had stopped taking my medicine for the last few months; it was like I could not prevent all of the words that were spilling out of my mouth to her. If I did not tell someone soon about what had happened to me, I felt that my head might explode.

She seemed relieved after I told her this because she informed me that she had suspected that I had stopped taking the risperidone and clozapine a while ago, and she asked me if my symptoms had come back. I told her that they had and that they were getting pretty intense, but I did not tell her anything else, and I especially told her nothing about the white van. After this, we talked for a very long time. She strongly encouraged me to tell my parents that night, and if I failed to do so, she informed me, she would tell them herself. As I mentioned, I play the saxophone and have since the fifth grade. I had a small concert coming up that Sunday at my high school in which I very much wanted to play. She agreed to not tell my parents that night, and I agreed that the two of us would tell my mom and dad on Sunday after the concert.

At this point, I essentially accepted the fact that I was most likely going to have to go back to the University of Michigan's psychiatric hospital and that I would have to then face my parents and Dr. Thomas with the fact that I had lied to them for so many months, but I felt I was ready and needed something to change. I was mentally exhausted from putting on the appearance of being okay when inside I was reeling with all kinds of pain I had never felt before and the ever-growing feeling that I was losing my hold on reality altogether. I was reluctantly willing to once again go back on some sort of medication—as long as it was not risperidone or clozapine.

Sunday came, and I played in the jazz band during the annual Taste Fest that my old high school used to host every year. After the concert was over, I told some of my very close friends in the band to talk to our band director the next day at school and let him know that I was not going to be in class for maybe a week or so. I very briefly explained to them that I was going to go home and drop a bombshell on my parents and that I was most likely going to go into the psychiatric hospital that night. All of them knew about my situation and wished me the best of luck. It is good to have friends like the ones I have.

I arrived at home after the concert, and with my girlfriend right next to me, I told my parents that I needed to talk to them about something. I explained to them that I had stopped taking the risperidone and clozapine and all the other medications that were designed to help with the side effects months ago. They seemed shocked, yet they were very understanding, which was an amazing support for me at that painful time in my life, and I felt very loved.

After many tears and many hugs, we packed up some of my clothes into a duffle bag, and we all headed out towards the University of Michigan Hospital, and even my little brother and my girlfriend came this time. It was around eight or eight thirty at night when we arrived at the hospital and made our way to the psychiatric emergency room.

It was another very long wait in the waiting room, and I went through the same procedure as the first time I was admitted to the psychiatric unit. First came speaking with a social worker and then with a resident doctor, with about a four-hour wait in between. Finally, at about one o'clock in the morning or so, I was led up to the children's psychiatric ward, as I was still seventeen at the time. I would again be the oldest patient in the unit, and I wondered if the nurses would still remember me.

Chapter 5
Shiny Metal Mirrors

The nurses did remember me. The night I was admitted, I was escorted past the nurse's station, and the night attendant recognized me immediately. She greeted me with mixed feelings. She told me, "No offense, but I hoped I would never have to see you in here again." And after another visual body inspection and after all the belongings I had in my pockets were placed in a holding box and another blood test (still with all negative results for street drugs), I was led to a room where a bed awaited me, and I fell into it without hesitation and fell fast asleep.

As I mentioned earlier, I was seventeen during both of my stays in the hospital, and therefore I was admitted to the child and adolescent unit of the University of Michigan's psychiatric hospital. Both times, I was the oldest patient in the unit with the other patients' ages ranging anywhere from five years old to young teenagers, and it was because I was the oldest in the unit that I formed very good relationships with the nurses and other staff members each time I was a patient there.

Each morning I was given a new team of nurses who would work in conjunction with Dr. Thomas, who also did a lot of work with inpatients as well as outpatients. This team of nurses and doctors were around the unit all day, and they made sure that I made it to the different activities that the staff had scheduled in which the patients were to participate. These activities began every morning at about seven thirty when I and all the other patients were woken up for breakfast. After that, the older patients were led to a small conference room that had been turned into a makeshift class-room with a decent amount of donated schoolbooks and a few old computers. The teacher who worked with the patients every morning was a volunteer, and she was the only staff member in the unit with whom I did not get along well.

The first time I was hospitalized, the main focus of the first couple of days was for me to get an MRI of my brain as soon as possible to rule out the possibility that the symptoms I was experiencing were the product of a brain tumor or any other physiological problem. This was obviously the only thing on my mind at that time, and I was not exactly happy to have to wake up so early every morning and go to this classroom and be bothered by this lady who would try to make me read chapters of some random textbook and have me take notes on it. I did not like the fact that I was given all these busy little tasks to accomplish every morning, and it seemed like a pretty big waste of a couple of hours each day.

The second time I was hospitalized, I got into a little argument with the volunteer teacher, and it ended up with me in the "quiet room," which translates to the "padded room." The argument began because of an incident with a young girl, probably around twelve or thirteen years old, who was under constant suicide watch. She had apparently previously attempted to take her own life, and she had carved the phrase "F*** off and die" *all* over her body with a razor or some other sharp blade. The volunteer teacher had assigned this young girl to the task of completing a small packet of workbook pages from a random grammar book, and the young patient was having many problems completing the assignment because the new medicine she had just begun taking the previous day was making it hard for her to think clearly and stay awake.

The teacher began to raise her voice when the young girl on suicide watch began to fall asleep at the table, and so the poor girl started crying. I was not exactly thrilled to be in the classroom in the first place, and watching the volunteer teacher make this young, unstable girl cry put me over the edge. I stood up and, without raising my voice, asked the teacher what exactly she thought she was doing, and then I informed her that it would probably be much better for everyone present if she just stopped talking to this patient altogether.

Needless to say, the teacher did not take too kindly to my suggestion, and she paged Sam, who was assigned to be my nurse for the day. Sam and I had easily gotten along both the first time I was admitted and also during the second time, and I did not want to give him any trouble when he showed up to the classroom and asked to speak with me in the hallway. He informed me that because of my little conversation with the teacher, I would have to go to the quiet room for forty-five minutes. Sam was a very nice guy, and he even went to my room and brought me a blanket and pillow so that I could take a little nap. I remember that I even considered having a little verbal scuffle with the teacher the next day if it meant that I could go to the quiet room and have a little extra sleep every morning, but I did not take this course of action as it was obviously a bad idea when the rest of the staff was so nice and helpful.

I got along very well with the rest of the nursing staff, and I met with Dr. Thomas every day. It was difficult for me to tell Dr. Thomas about all of the months that I had lied to him and everyone about taking my medications, but he was very understanding about the whole situation. He informed me that I was not in trouble in any way, and that if I ever felt like going off my medicine again, I should consult him first, and we could then make a decision about medication changes.

After "school" was done each morning, the rest of the day was spent in group therapy sessions where we older patients had our own more adult discussions than the group of younger patients. I made a lot of friends during these sessions, and I learned a great deal about other types of mental disorders and how people deal with them. We were not supposed to ask any of the other patients about why they were in the psychiatric unit, but that did not stop me from talking about my personal experiences with anyone who wanted to know about them during these group sessions and during the three meals every day. I did not, however, tell anyone about the incident involving the white van; I would not be ready to tell anyone else about that night for a while.

When there was no group discussion scheduled, the middle of the day was usually spent doing some sort of arts and crafts project, and I did many paintings during these times and also got to know many of the other patients. After the arts and crafts room was closed up for the day, it would usually be around lunchtime, so we would all go to the cafeteria room and have lunch. No matter where we went, there was always at least one nurse with us at all times, and I thought it was nice of the nurses to eat with us. I struck up many conversations with them during the times of the day when there was not much going on, and this way I got to know many of them and the time passed much quicker than it would have had I no one to talk to.

The nurses generally liked me because, as they told me, they did not often get patients in the unit who were older and/or capable of speaking with them as adults. They were all very encouraging and good sources of strength and advice when things seemed bad, and this especially proved true during my first hospitalization.

The evenings and nights were free time, and I would usually go to the "day room," which housed the big television and all the coloring books and crayons you could possibly imagine. During my second hospitalization, I very quickly made friends with a five-year-old girl during this free time who decided that I was her coloring buddy just about the second she first saw me.

I will never forget that little girl for as long as I live. Her name was Danielle, and she was a perfectly normal and healthy five-year-old who was full of energy and curiosity, as people of that age are. The only thing that kept her in the children's psychiatric unit instead of preschool was the fact that she would compulsively pull individual strands of her hair out and eat them. Her parents would come every evening and find her dragging me around by the hand playing some high-energy imagination game with stuffed animals or coloring some princess in a coloring book, and I quickly became friends with Danielle's mom and dad too.

It was not very long before I began to miss my saxophone, so I asked the nursing staff if my parents could bring her to the unit so that I could practice during free time. They asked around with the doctors, and everyone determined that it would be fine, so I called my parents and asked them to bring Charlene (my saxophone) with them the next time they came to visit. It took no more than a few practice sessions before the nurses suggested that I put on a miniature concert for the rest of the patients, which was arranged to be held in the day room the next evening, so I began practicing the old book of Disney songs that I still have from grade school. The parents and the other patients, especially the younger ones, seemed to enjoy the little recital, and I became even closer with the nurses and other staff members.

It was altogether a very interesting and different experience for me to have stayed in a psychiatric unit a total of two times. It was a much different atmosphere than anywhere else I have ever been, and that fact was driven home for me the first time I took a shower during my first hospitalization.

I automatically attempted to lock the door behind myself after I had stepped into the bathroom and had removed all of my clothes, but there was no lock. There were no locks on any of the patients' room doors, and this is obviously because the nurses need to be able to get to the patients in case of an emergency.

Jim Stallings

I looked up while standing in front of the sink to brush my teeth, and I was looking at myself in a shiny metal mirror. There was no glass in any of the patients' rooms because it was a hazard in the case of a suicidal patient who might break the glass in order to cut him or herself.

During my first stay in the unit, the first morning I was awake and having breakfast, the nurse who was in the cafeteria room with us noticed that I was wearing a belt, which is also not allowed. She calmly told me that I would have to take the belt off and give it to her, so I stood up to comply, but as I reached for it, she told me rather sternly to stop.

She informed me that she would have to be the one who would take the belt off of me and that I should put my hands up in the air. I gave her a weird look and put my hands up while two other nurses slowly surrounded me and blocked off any exit route I had to the doorway. She carefully removed my belt and told me that she would place it in the box that held the rest of my belongings, including my watch, necklace, and shoelaces.

How I Lost My Mind and Found Myself

It was a bit of a hard transition for me going from living at home and then being in a psychiatric unit. Before the two experiences I had while I was an inpatient, I had never before been in a situation where I was forced to stay behind locked doors. Just the mere fact that I could not leave to go anywhere when I wanted was a huge difference from my life as a high school student and a fully licensed driver.

After a patient is in the child and adolescent psychiatric unit for over twenty-four hours, the doctors and nurses assigned to that patient get together and decide whether or not the patient is eligible for a parent or other nursing staff member to take him or her out of the unit to go anywhere on hospital grounds for up to two hours. I never had any trouble obtaining this status as I was never considered to be a flight risk or dangerous to myself or anyone else, and my parents would often escort me outside or downstairs to the cafeteria to get some higher quality lunch and dinner.

The second time I was hospitalized, a group of my friends came and visited me when my dad and I were wandering around outside getting some fresh air. It made me feel so much better about my situation to see them, and the poster they made me still hangs on the wall in my bedroom alongside all the stuffed animals and cards they brought to cheer me up. During the second time I was in the unit, my dad even went so far as to take me out to a nice restaurant in downtown Ann Arbor, which was a big risk, but it was absolutely worth it. I do not know how much longer I could have survived on hospital food alone.

Twenty-four hours into my second stay in the hospital, Dr. Thomas suggested that I go on a newer medication called aripiprazole (Abilify). This particular drug, like the others in the antipsychotic family, takes a long time to build up effective levels in a person's bloodstream, but the side effects are reported to not be as severe as some of the other antipsychotic drugs. I was going to have to take the aripiprazole twice a day along with the other medications that were designed to help lessen its side effects.

Some of the side effects with aripiprazole that were described on the piece of paper I was given about the drug include the following: fever; stiff muscles; confusion; sweating; fast or uneven heartbeats; jerky muscle movements that cannot be controlled; dry mouth; sudden numbness or weakness, especially on one side of the body; sudden headache; problems with vision, speech, or balance; increased thirst; excessive hunger; light-headedness; fainting; and urinating less or not at all. Along with this list of side effects and additional information about aripiprazole, Dr. Thomas also warned me about a condition called akathisia, which is a movement disorder that is characterized by restlessness, a compelling need for constant movement, bouncing feet, and rocking back and forth. That side effect was the worst one of all for me while I was taking the aripiprazole, and I felt it the hardest during the week while I was still in the hospital waiting to be released.

Like the other medications I was taking, I experienced many of the listed side effects of the aripiprazole. I experienced a lot of dry mouth and even more uncontrolled muscle movements, such as little spasms of the face and neck and slight but constant tremors in both of my hands. These side effects, like the ones I had previously experienced, made it extremely difficult to concentrate on anything and sit still. I would constantly be moving around, bouncing my feet, or rocking my body back and forth for hours and hours on end, which would often leave me feeling physically exhausted at the end of the day.

Like my first hospitalization, my second stay in the unit was for a week, and after that week was over, I was more than ready to get back to school and back to my life. I had received a brand new medication to try out and a brand new diagnosis as well.

To be clinically and formally diagnosed with schizophrenia, a patient has to meet a few guidelines as outlined by the DSM IV, which stands for the *Diagnostic and Statistical Manual of Mental Disorders*, a book that can be found on the desk of any psychiatrist or psychologist. The guidelines outlined in the DSM IV for a diagnosis of schizophrenia are as follows:

A. Characteristic symptoms are two or more of the following for at least one month:
    1. Delusions
    2. Hallucinations
    3. Disorganized speech
    4. Grossly disorganized or catatonic behavior
    5. Negative symptoms, including flattened or blunted emotions
B. Social or occupational dysfunction
C. Symptoms persist for at least six months
D. Does not show signs of manic-depressive behavior or other significant mood episodes
E. Substance abuse exclusion
F. No relationship to a pervasive developmental disorder, such as autism

As you can see, I fit the bill quite well, and it was not hard for Dr. Thomas to formally diagnose me with paranoid schizophrenia after my second stay in the hospital. Before my second hospitalization, Dr. Thomas had suggested that he believed that the symptoms I was describing to him and my parents were those characteristic of schizophrenia, but the duration of those symptoms had not yet lasted at least six months.

So after another stay at the University of Michigan, I was free to go. I was on another antipsychotic medication, and I would again have to deal with its side effects. I did not, however, tell anyone about the incident involving the white van. I was not yet ready to share that bit of information with anyone, not even Dr. Thomas, and this was mostly because I was terrified of the reactions my friends and family would have if I told them that I recently had believed that I had shot a man to death.

Things were looking better to me though. I was happy to have at least some sort of stability in my life again, and I was looking forward to getting back to school and seeing all of my friends. I was still hearing voices every now and then, but I had not seen Douglas since before my hospital stay. It seemed that the aripiprazole was making my hallucinations fewer and somewhat far between, but they definitely were not gone.

How I Lost My Mind and Found Myself

The side effects of the aripiprazole were different than those of the risperidone and clozapine, and they were less severe. But even though the side effects of the aripiprazole did not completely drain me of my mental abilities, the restlessness due to the akathisia was terrible. I could not sit still, not even for a moment, and this inability to control my movements made it nearly impossible for me to do the things I loved, such as playing the saxophone. It became extremely hard for me to sit through classes or to read because I was experiencing this constant need to move that was brought on by the akathisia.

But all in all, I desperately needed a change from the terrible thoughts and fears that had been tearing me apart inside during the last few weeks of summer and into the school year. I was feeling good at that time about my decision to go back into the hospital and back on medication, and I worked hard to deal with the side effects of the aripiprazole so that I could perform well in school and at home. Things were beginning to look relatively good for the time being.

Chapter 6
Round Two

So, shortly after my senior year of high school began, I was once again taking antipsychotic medication every day, and I was once again finding it hard to concentrate and perform well in my classes. Before I knew it, my grades began slipping, and it was quickly becoming harder and harder for me to pay attention fully during classes. I also found it to be quite difficult to even stay awake for most of the day.

I was continuing to se Dr. Thomas about once every week or so, and I was open and honest with him about my symptoms and the side effects I was experiencing from the aripiprazole. I continued to hear voices often during this time period, and Douglas came to visit me briefly two weeks after I was released from the psychiatric unit. When Douglas showed up randomly in my house one evening while I was alone and watching television, I relied heavily on

Jim Stallings

the techniques to determine whether or not something is real that were suggested to me by the University of Michigan nursing staff and the other inpatients.

Douglas came into the living room from behind where I was lying on the couch and began speaking to me while he was standing off to my right-hand side. He told me that he had come just to talk to me about my hospitalization and what I had told the nurses and doctors about him while I was locked in the unit. I ignored him completely—or as completely as I could manage—until someone else walked into the room. After a couple of minutes of silence, Douglas became very upset with me and began shouting. John, my little brother, walked into the room and sat down next to me on the couch shortly after Douglas began his ranting. I noticed that John did not pay Douglas any attention whatsoever as he calmly asked me what I was watching.

That was the first time I began to fight back, so to speak, against the hallucinations that had become the toughest roadblocks in my life. I experimented for a very long time with the different strategies I employ

88

nowadays in order to control myself while I am in the midst of a psychotic episode, and that first experiment with the use of ignoring my hallucinations altogether was a great personal success for me. John had no idea that I was hallucinating a shouting and very angry Douglas right next to him on the couch that evening.

But it would still be a number of months of taking my medications and dealing with the hallucinations before I would feel confident enough to stop taking the pills altogether. The second round of medications while I was working to complete my senior year of high school was to become my proving and testing grounds for the rest of my life.

But merely completing my senior year of high school would prove very difficult for me. The aripiprazole, although not as bad as the risperidone and clozapine in terms of side effects, adversely affected the way in which I thought and solved problems, and soon my grades became an issue for the second time in my life. I had always been a slightly above average student, and I now saw my grade point average slipping, which I had worked so hard to build over the previous three years. Coupled with the akathisia and the general restlessness that was, in my personal case, the aripiprazole's worst side effect, I could not get assignments done on time, and what proved worse than that, the first semester finals were quickly approaching, as well as the deadlines for college applications.

The first semester of my senior year of high school was the last semester of grades that would be sent to the colleges I had applied to with the rest of my transcripts, and I needed to do well on all of my finals. I would get together with my friends, and we would all study in someone's basement for hours and hours. I estimate that I completed anywhere from eight to twelve hours of study time for each final, and when I finally got my grades over Christmas break, the news was not so good.

I had ended up failing two of my finals and doing poorly on the others. I remember that I had been so frustrated when I took the exams because I knew that I had studied all of the material well in advance and very extensively, but when it came to test time, I could not for the life of me access the information I had studied and memorized. My thought processes had taken a big hit from the aripiprazole, and I was feeling like I was beginning to revert back into that old, horrible zombie shell of myself that I was when I was on the risperidone and clozapine.

I knew some pretty big changes had to be made, but I also knew that I was in no way ready to go completely off my medications at that time without risking another possible life-altering event like the one I had with Douglas and the white van. After thinking everything over for the rest of the Christmas break, I decided to go back and finish the school year as best as I could while dealing with the side effects of the aripiprazole.

All of my teachers knew about my situation and so did a good portion of the student body after I returned from the hospital the second time. All of my teachers were more than willing to help me out in any way that they could with assignments and even offered to give me extra time to complete quizzes and tests, but I always politely refused. This may seem like a pretentious thing to do, but I never once needed or wanted to be treated any differently because of my diagnosis. I took my failed final grades and had my guidance counselor send them to the colleges that I applied for, even though he offered to send them the recalculated grade point average I would have had if the failed grades were factored out. I was not, nor am I still, looking for any handouts or anything that would put me at what I consider to be an unfair advantage over my fellow students or colleagues.

And believe me, I have heard it all: "But Jim, it's not like this is your fault. If you had cancer and were on chemotherapy, we wouldn't expect you to run a marathon." Or my personal favorite: "But Jim, it's not your fault. If you had diabetes, everyone would understand if you couldn't go out and eat certain kinds of foods or have too much sugar."

That all sounds nice, but I do not have cancer or diabetes; I have schizophrenia, which I assure you is completely different. It was during this time in my life when I began to really grow as a person, and I began to realize and become comfortable with who I am. I knew that in order to have people not treat me any differently than before, which is what I wanted, I had to apply that same attitude to myself; I was honestly okay, and even proud to some degree, to send the colleges a failed test score that took me twelve hours of studying to earn. If that is what I worked so hard to earn, that is what I got, and at least I could look myself in the mirror and know that I gave it my best shot.

Luckily, I was able to finish my senior year of high school and graduate in the standard four years from Detroit Catholic Central High School with a raised grade point average of about a 3.2, which I could certainly live with. I was accepted into Michigan State University and would be heading off there in the fall of 2005. I am very thankful for all the help that my dad provided me with when I was filling out my college applications. I was having great difficulty focusing on them, and my dad helped me out with this problem immensely and with an amazing, saint-like patience.

Jim Stallings

He knew that I was having a very, very difficult time concentrating on anything, so he and I would get together on the weekends and fill out the online applications soon after they were made available to hopeful students. Anyone who has ever filled out an application to attend a college or university knows exactly how tricky they can be. Thanks to my dad, I got all my applications in early, and he provided me with immense amounts of help on the essay portions and helped me focus and concentrate in order to complete them.

It was the second semester of my senior year that I came out, so to speak, with my diagnosis to the entire school, and this was the time when I wrote my short story based on my experiences and gave it to my family and some of my friends. I was also taking a psychology course that semester, and I approached my teacher and told him about my past experiences and told him some information about the two times I was hospitalized and what medications I was taking at the time. I also informed him that I would be more than happy to give him a copy of my short story that I had recently written and that I would also be fine with speaking to the entire class about my experiences. He somewhat reluctantly agreed to let me do just that. When our class came to the chapters that dealt with abnormal psychology and mental disorders, I printed off enough copies of my short story so that everyone in the class could have one, and I spoke in front of them, detailing my past and answering any of their questions.

Towards the end of my senior year, things were looking much better to me, and I was excited for the fall to arrive when I would be going off to Michigan State, which was where most of my close friends from high school were going as well. I was still taking the aripiprazole, but Dr. Thomas was starting to wonder if a medication change would be in my best interest.

He got the idea to make some changes in my medications after he read my short story, which I wrote one night about three or four months before my senior year ended. I felt I was finally ready to get the incident with the white van off of my chest and let my family and friends know more fully about me, and I was tired of the "Dear

Diary" entries that Dr. Thomas wanted me to write whenever I experienced any symptoms.

Dr. Thomas was concerned with some of the language I had used in my short story when describing how I was feeling at particular times. He thought that I might be experiencing some sort of mania coupled with the psychotic symptoms I was describing.

"He [I] felt as though he were seeing for the first time, feeling for the first time. How could he resist going out into that dark, cold world? As he left the comfortable front hallway of his house and stepped into the night, Damian felt like a god." Passages like that led Dr. Thomas to believe that maybe I was experiencing some sort of manic symptoms, so he suggested that I begin taking another drug called semisodium valproate (Depakote) in combination with the aripiprazole and the medications designed to help me with the side effects.

semisodium valproate is a mood stabilizer and is often given to people who have bipolar disorder, which is also known as manic-depressive disorder, a disorder that can cause intense mood swings ranging from incredible highs to terrible, debilitating depressions. It is also used to treat different types of seizure disorders, such as epilepsy. Dr. Thomas thought the semisodium valproate might help, so I agreed and decided to give it a try. Some of the side effects of semisodium valproate that were listed on the piece of paper Dr. Thomas gave me to read over include the following: unexplained weakness, vomiting, confusion, fainting, easy bruising or bleeding, fever, skin rash, swollen glands, chills, body aches, flu-like symptoms, urinating less than usual, blood in the urine, hallucinations, lack of coordination, extreme drowsiness, weight gain, double vision, and back and forth movements of the eyes.

I was beginning to see a pattern in the side effects of the different medications I was now taking every day, and I did not like it. I was hesitant to begin taking semisodium valproate after reading that lengthy list of side effects and coupling it with the list of side effects that goes along with aripiprazole, but Dr. Thomas really believed that the semisodium valproate might help me.

So I added semisodium valproate to the aripiprazole and the other drugs I was taking to combat their side effects and went back to school with even more side effects to deal with. At this point in my life, I was getting pretty tired of spending my days drugged out of my mind by medications that were designed to make me somehow "normal." But I did not want to put my friends and especially not my family though another episode like the one I had when I secretly stopped taking the risperidone and clozapine over the summer and during the beginning of my senior year. With that lengthy and extremely draining episode in mind, I took the aripiprazole and semisodium valproate every day, and they did to some small degree slow the frequency of my usual auditory and visual hallucinations, but they were definitely not anything close to a miracle cure.

After about a month and a half, I began to notice that I was rapidly gaining weight and that it was nearly impossible for me to drop this weight. I was a member of the shot put and discus throwing team my sophomore, junior, and senior years of high school, and I was lifting weights and exercising a great deal with the rest of the team, but I was not gaining muscle weight—I was just getting pudgy. The other side effects that I experienced from the aripiprazole seemed to be heightened by the addition of semisodium valproate, and I was not feeling particularly good about my medication situation by the time my senior year ended.

During the first month of summer, I approached Dr. Thomas one of our sessions and told him that I was unhappy with the semisodium valproate and that I was still experiencing hallucinations on a regular basis. He told me that I should stop taking the semisodium valproate, most likely fearing that I would secretly go off of my medications again if he did not support me. Dr. Thomas then suggested that I instead begin taking an antipsychotic drug called haloperidol (Haldol) along with the aripiprazole.

Haldol is an older medication and is one of the first in the antipsychotic family to be widely used on patients. It was invented and first used in 1957, and it became FDA approved in the United States in 1988. I would now be taking the oldest and the newest antipsychotic medications at the same time, which was something Dr. Thomas pointed out to me when he gave me a piece of paper outlining some of the side effects of haloperidol. Those side effects include the following: headache; blurred vision; faster than normal heartbeat; dry mouth; difficulty sleeping; drowsiness; confusion; Kellie is cool; blood disorders; abnormal heartbeats; low blood pressure; seizures; urinary hesitancy; abnormal movements of the hands, legs, face, neck, and tongue; tremors; twitching; rigidity; increased salivation; high blood prolactin levels; uncontrolled rolling of the eyes or neck; fever; sweating; anxiety; restlessness; constipation; vomiting; and abdominal pain.

The side effects of haloperidol that I experienced were terrible. I had become accustomed to the hand tremors and the random twitches that I experienced while on the aripiprazole, but the added effects of the haloperidol made them much worse. Once the haloperidol had built up enough in my bloodstream to become effective, my arms and legs began twitching, and it was quickly becoming almost impossible for me to stay awake. I even remember falling asleep during a conversation with one of my friends while she was in the middle of a sentence.

During the first month that I spent on summer vacation, Dr. Thomas was tying up any loose ends that he had because he was preparing to move out to Colorado at the end of the month. Because he would be leaving and therefore no longer able to treat me, he wished to transfer my care over to a psychiatrist at Michigan State University, preferably someone who had a practice on campus. After Dr. Thomas had searched around for a short time and gotten in contact with people he knew in East Lansing, we decided that my care would be transferred over to Dr. Black, who was a practicing psychiatrist at the OLIN Health Center on Michigan State's campus. But before Dr. Thomas left for Colorado, he asked me to do him one last favor.

When I gave Dr. Thomas a copy of my short story, I also gave him my permission to

Jim Stallings

give the story to anyone he wanted—colleagues or students or whomever. He told
me that he had given my story to twelve
fourth-year medical students he was in-
structing and evaluating a few times a
week, and he asked me if I would be willing to get together with all of them and
speak to them about my short story. I happily agreed as I figured that I could help a
panel of future child and adolescent psychiatrists, and I felt that I could offer them
some real-world advice that they could
then apply to their patients one day.

So a few weeks before Dr. Thomas left,
we got together with the twelve medical
students in a conference room down the
hall from his office. We ended up speaking about many different topics pertain-
ing to my symptoms, and I answered their
questions for about three hours. It felt good
to me to get out there and talk to people
about my experiences with schizophrenia,
and I promised myself multiple times that
summer that I would spread my personal
story to as many people as I could.

However, I was still fighting the side effects of my medications. Instead of making

102

anything better for me, the combination of aripiprazole and haloperidol caused by far the worst side effects I had ever experienced. I was only on the two drugs for about the first month of the summer after I graduated from high school before I decided that enough was enough. I had been on too many medications, all of them being extremely high doses, and I had been a drugged-out-of-my-mind zombie for far too long. To me, it seemed like curing allergies by putting the allergic person in a coma. Sure that person might not be bothered by his or her allergies, but now he or she is in a coma. It did not seem like a fair trade to me.

I was seeing Dr. Black at the OLIN Health Center at Michigan State about once a week after Dr. Thomas left for Colorado. My dad and I would drive about an hour from my house over to East Lansing to go to my appointments, and often my dad would be in the room. After a few appointments with Dr. Black, I informed her that I would no longer be taking any medications whatsoever.

Jim Stallings

I arrived at this decision after many months of testing myself while I was hallucinating. I had gotten to the point where people did not even notice when I was hearing voices or seeing Douglas, and I, and even my dad, felt that it was time to give not taking any medication a try. Needless to say, Dr. Black was not happy about my decision, and she pressed me to begin taking some other medication during each and every appointment we had. She became much more aggressive in her approach to try and get me to start up another medication regimen after she read my short story, as you can well imagine.

After about two weeks of kicking my medication to the curb, I was feeling better than ever. I could think again, my hands had stopped constantly trembling, I could sit still and focus on a book for more than thirteen seconds, and I could again urinate when and where I wanted—life was good. I did hallucinate more, and though I was not necessarily able to control them, I found that I was much more able to react to them positively, and I quickly learned to live alongside the voices that spoke to me every day. I even grew accustomed to seeing Douglas every now and then and completely ignoring him.

Dr. Black could never really appreciate what I was doing for myself though, and I believe that it was her strict psychiatrist background that made her predict some pretty horrible outcomes of my decision to not take medication. She repeatedly told me that without medication, I would relapse into a psychotic state and have to be hospitalized by the end of the semester, if not before, and she was constantly telling me about the risk of suicide, which I have never in my life considered an option.

I did not feel the same way as she did about my new self-treatment. I especially did not share those same feelings after spending about four months medication-free and now fully adjusted to dormitory and college life at Michigan State and doing and feeling quite well. In early November of my freshman year in college, I stopped going to see Dr. Black altogether.

The decision to stop seeing Dr. Black came pretty easily to me. Every appointment we had, she would tell me that I needed to be on this medication or that medication, and if I did not take the medication, I would spend the rest of my natural life in and out of mental institutions; I was quickly becoming quite sick of this nonsense. I was getting good grades, socializing successfully with many people, forging lasting relationships, living in a dorm with a good friend of mine with no problems, and in general, I was feeling awesome about my situation. I figured that she could take the hour a week that she was *not* helping me with anything and use that time to help some other patient who might actually benefit from talking to her.

I kind of feel bad, but at the same time not really, because I did not tell Dr. Black I was not going to come to our appointments anymore; I just simply stopped going and stopped calling her. Whenever the receptionist would call me and tell me that I needed to make another appointment with Dr. Black, I would always tell her some excuse like I was just about to walk into a class or just sitting down for a bite of lunch and that I would call her right back to reschedule, but I never did. I know this seems

How I Lost My Mind and Found Myself

kind of mean and inconsiderate, but I felt like I was finally breaking away from that portion of my life and that I was on the right path towards the rest of it. I was done with medication and ready to start my life as the new, although slightly crazier, me.

Chapter 7
Under the Influence

All of the antipsychotic medications that I was prescribed back in high school interact with specific parts or specific chemicals in the brain. Some work to block certain chemicals, such as serotonin or dopamine, and some interact with different neurotransmitters and their pathways, which are found deep within the brain's nervous tissues.

Antipsychotic medications are currently classified into two categories, first generation and second generation, which are sometimes referred to as typical and atypical antipsychotic medications. These drugs also do not act to "cure" schizophrenia or the number of other disorders that they are prescribed for; rather, they act, hopefully, to control a patient's symptoms and make life for that individual better overall, more enjoyable, and more manageable. First-generation antipsychotics are categorized

Jim Stallings

into five different chemical families depending on the drug's high, intermediate, or low potency. The potency is dependent on how high of a dose of a particular drug a patient needs in order to safely produce the desired effect.

The second-generation antipsychotic medications have had a profound effect on the prescriptions that clinical psychiatrists have been using to treat their patients ever since their release. In 1997, it was reported that half of patients with schizophrenia were taking second-generation antipsychotic medications, and by 2005, the number of patients who were taking these medications reached over two-thirds. This change from the first generation to the second is largely believed to have happened because the second-generation medications often have fewer or less harsh side effects than their first-generation predecessors. As I mentioned, I personally have taken both first- and second-generation antipsychotics, and for a while I took both first- and second-generation medications at the same time; I generally reacted better to the second-generation antipsychotics, as do most other patients.

The first-generation antipsychotic medication that I have taken is haloperidol; risperidone, clozapine, and aripiprazole are all second-generation medications. The semisodium valproate that I was prescribed is classified as a mood stabilizer and therefore does not fall into the category of either a first or a second-generation antipsychotic medication.

The first-generation medications were created to focus mainly either on the dopamine receptors, more specifically the receptors for dopamine-2, and the serotonin receptors in the brain. They act in most cases to block these receptor sites. This action is generally thought to suppress the psychotic symptoms that a patient might have due to an over actively stimulated brain because large levels of dopamine or serotonin are present and work to stimulate the parts of the brain that are responsible for sight, hearing, and sensing, thus producing hallucinations.

Second-generation antipsychotic medications generally interact with different neurotransmitters that send chemical messages all throughout the brain. These neurotransmitters send the messages through the tiny synapses between the nerve cells and are responsible for our ability to see, hear, and in general to experience the world in a "normal" manner. The second-generation medications work to fix, regulate, and restore any synapses that might have become damaged within the brain, causing a patient to see, hear, or experience things that are not real due to the fact the chemical messages are being interpreted incorrectly by the patient's brain.

As you can see, these drugs act to interfere with the mechanisms that the patient's brain uses in order to form the delusions and hallucinations that a person with schizophrenia or any other psychotic disorder experiences. When these mechanisms—the dopamine and serotonin receptors or neurotransmitters—are altered by these drugs, the side effects can be devastating and debilitating, as I have outlined in previous chapters. When taking these medications, it felt to me like someone had transplanted a whole new brain into my head, a brain that I was not used to using, and it felt extremely uncomfortable and unnatural to me.

I currently see a doctor who is not a psychiatrist, but a humanistic psychologist, and she also is someone who does not believe in medicating patients to the point of being uncomfortable. In my personal experience, psychiatrists are a lot more ready and willing to prescribe the medications that are used to treat mental patients. I, however, prefer a more humanistic approach to my situation.

These days, I especially do not appreciate having different medications pushed on me by anyone, and for me to finally have found a doctor who promotes my not taking medication has been a wonderful treat for me. My current doctor has told me that she much prefers helping her patients work through their problems without the use of medication and that she would much rather suggest vitamins, minerals, and other natural supplements that have shown signs of helping patients in the past, as well as behavioral and cognitive therapies. We have had many fantastic sessions during which I have learned a great deal of information about the different fields of psychology and psychiatry, and she has helped me to overcome some tough problems that I have faced recently, all without the constant doses of medications.

For my first two hospitalizations and the months on the medications that followed in between and after, there were no other treatment options made known or available to me other than the antipsychotic drugs. I now know that I do in fact have a choice as to the manner in which my treatment will to be handled. A lifetime of medication every day is not anything I am interested in, and it can also lead to some serious health problems. I have briefly outlined the side effect from the aripiprazole that is called akathisia, which is a movement disorder and one that set me back in school and at home a great deal.

Not only can these drugs—both first-generation and second-generation medications—cause movement disorders in patients, they can also cause lasting liver and heart problems, such as an increase

114

or decrease in blood pressure for the rest of a patient's life, regardless of whether he or she continues taking the drug. Luckily, I experienced no lasting side effects or health problems due to my years of taking the different medications, but other patients are not as lucky as I am.

I consider myself very lucky to have been diagnosed with schizophrenia in this day and age. People who suffered from some form of mental illness in the past typically had a much harder time in life than people do today considering the treatments they were often forced to endure. Many people in different ancient cultures who exhibited what we would today call symptoms of mental illness were often regarded as divinely inspired by their societies, and they were often greatly respected as holy people, shamans, and prophets. In Europe in the mid-eighteenth through the late nineteenth century, however, all that changed for the worse.

People who exhibited signs of "madness," as it was commonly referred to during that time period, were often subjected to torments that were later said to rival those faced by the millions of Jews who suffered and died in the many Nazi concentration camps during World War II. Many, many people were kept in cages completely naked, fastened to a wall with iron chains, and given very little food.

Some of the other popular treatment options during the mid-eighteenth through the late nineteenth century in Europe were the techniques of bloodletting and the seemingly all-purpose, cure-all lobotomy. Patients who were confined to psychiatric hospitals were oftentimes believed to be possessed by some sort of demonic spirit, especially if the patient was prone to violence and lots of shouting. In this case, the treatment was that he or she would be restrained by the use of chains, and prayers would be recited by the "doctors" and any other religious individual present as gashes were made in the abdomen of the patient in the shape of a cross. Many patients reportedly lost their lives to this highly painful form of treatment due to extreme loss of blood. The bloodletting was said to cleanse the body of any demonic forces that were at work within the patient that were thought to be the cause of the person's symptoms. Those who administered this treatment never intervened to stop the bleeding as it was believed that it was up to God to stop the bleeding only after all the demons or evil spirits had been successfully cast out of the patient's body.

Patients of this time period were also administered lobotomies. A lobotomy is a medical procedure during which the skull is punctured by a sharp, pointed instrument in strategic places in order to produce the desired effect of lessening or curing a mental patient's symptoms. This procedure was not limited only to the mid-eighteenth through the late nineteenth century Europeans, and it has been used quite extensively in modern times as well. For instance, John F. Kennedy's younger sister was publicly known to have mental retardation, and she later in her life developed schizophrenia and underwent a lobotomy.

The American state-funded psychiatric hospitals were widely regarded as some of the most wretched places in the country when the conditions the patients of these institutions had to contend with every day were made public by a number of articles published shortly after World War II. Magazines such as *Life* and *Reader's Digest* as well as many nonfiction books and newspaper reports shed light on the horrifying and inhumane conditions of the state-funded psychiatric hospitals during that time period. Extremely undernourished patients were photographed huddled together completely naked in filthy corridors, and many reports of the high death tolls at these institutions were published with a special emphasis on the fact that no hospital worker was ever convicted of a crime or malpractice. It is largely due to President John F. Kennedy's understanding of mental illness and his personal knowledge of how schizophrenia can affect a close family member that we have updated, safe, and humane state-funded mental institutions today.

There is now a great deal of time, money, and interest going into the research, development, and marketing of new antipsychotic medications with some interesting and new avenues being explored. Nicotine-based antipsychotic medications are now being widely researched by many of the world's pharmaceutical companies and laboratories. These medications are thought to help greatly reduce the side effects of the drugs and help a patient with schizophrenia better control his or her symptoms. As more and more research and development goes into creating newer and better antipsychotic medications, the world will continue to become better and better for the millions of people who suffer from schizophrenia worldwide and rely on their medication.

Chapter 8
Good, F*** 'Em.

There were some people in my life who were very worried about my decision to tell many people that I have schizophrenia. My mom was at first against my decision to tell my fellow high school students by addressing my psychology class, but she has greatly changed her views about my decision since then.

Back in high school during my senior year a few days before I was scheduled to speak to my psychology class, a close friend of mine who knew that I was going to do this presentation asked me, "Aren't you worried that some people will treat you differently after they hear this about you? You know how some people just can't deal with stuff like this."

To which I replied, and pardon my French, "Good, f*** 'em."

That is the philosophy that I live my life by, and that three-word phrase has become my rock and my strength when I consider what other people will think of me when they find out that I have schizophrenia. In my opinion, if someone else cannot somehow deal with the fact that I am a schizophrenic, that is not my problem—that is their problem. And if that person is going to then act like a jerk, why would I ever want to go out of my way to impress someone like that? That's just the way I see things.

This is the attitude that I have been growing inside of me ever since I decided to tell people what is going on in my head. I believe that it is because of my personal philosophy of "Good, f*** 'em" that I can successfully discontinue taking any and all antipsychotic medications, not see a psychiatrist once a week, tell anyone who cares to know about my personal history, have many, many lasting friends at school and at home, and write a book detailing my experiences.

This philosophy came to me like a bolt of lightning, and it has changed my life for the better ever since. I realized a few years ago after I had graduated from high school that life is all about choices. The choices I was faced with back during that summer after my senior year were extremely different from each other. On the one hand, I could choose to stay on one or more antipsychotic medications and be drugged out of my mind and possibly spend the rest of my natural life in and out of some mental institution. Or I could not. I have way too many personal plans for the rest of my life to let a little thing like paranoid schizophrenia slow me down, even if my symptoms are considered to be fairly extreme by mental health professionals.

Many mental patients develop a feeling of being "trapped" by their diagnosis, which only adds to many people's problems. I understand all too well how these feelings can come about when it seems like everyone in the world is telling you that because of this or that diagnosis, you need to be on a certain medicine or combination of medicines in order to become and remain "normal." It feels like a cage is closing in around you.

These feelings only intensify when a person is subjected to hospitalization and

Jim Stallings

when many different doctors and other staff members continue to tell that patient that he or she is sick. And what are we told is the best way to cure an illness? Medicine. And I ask you to please understand that I am not preaching that giving mental patients medication is a bad thing at all, but in my personal case, it was, and at first, no other options were made known to me. I have seen medication of all sorts helping people with many different problems including depression, bipolar disorder, and schizophrenia, but I have tried out many different medications and many different combinations of them, and none of them have worked to help me.

I found a way to deal with any problems my schizophrenia can throw at me, and the way I did it was to stop taking my medication altogether. I formulated a new attitude about my situation based on the philosophy of "Good, f*** 'em," and I was feeling better and better about myself and my situation. I knew that I had made the right decisions and taken the right steps to get to where I wanted to be in my life. For the first time since I began to hear mysterious voices whispering to me when no one else was around, I felt very good about myself and my situation. I began to really discover who I am.

I also decided that I was going to reach out to anyone who wanted to know more about my experiences, and I decided to try and help as many people as I could. I had gone to a few group family therapy sessions at Dr. Thomas's old office over the summer following my graduation from high school, and I had met five different schizophrenics and their families. I was the youngest patient in the group, and my parents and oftentimes my brothers and friends would come with me to these sessions.

We would discuss all kinds of topics such as job retention, paying bills on time, and schizophrenia-related problems with other family members and their possible solutions. These were usually topics that I had little or no interest in during that time in my life when I was not yet a full-time member of the workforce and I did not have a mortgage to pay off, but I learned a lot about what other schizophrenics are like. I also learned that many other patients respond much better than I did to the antipsychotic medications that I had previously been taking.

I seemed to be the most talkative patient there, and I would oftentimes stay after everyone had left and speak with the two women who ran the sessions. I decided during those sessions that I would never let myself be afraid to tell anyone about my history with schizophrenia. I was always more than willing to talk about it with anyone, and at these sessions I realized that I did not seem to mind talking about my past history as much as the other patients did, who I assumed had been somewhat conditioned by years of taking medications and not telling many people about their situations, not to mention the social stigma that is attached to a diagnosis like schizophrenia.

I feel that because I was the youngest patient there, I had a much different perspective than the other people did about the diagnosis of schizophrenia. I was always suggesting that the group should talk to each other about why we were all there together, share past experiences with symptoms, and share stories about hospitaliza-tions, but this was always frowned upon by everyone else who was present.

There was a sort of a "don't ask, don't tell" policy when it came to everyone's past experiences, and I did not agree with that policy. I have never had a problem with anyone knowing about my personal history, even though I realize that the words "paranoid schizophrenia" are very scary words to many people.

Chapter 9
Very Scary Words

It is ridiculous to assume that there is not an automatic stigma that is attached to any mental patient following a diagnosis. I see it all the time on television, in movies, in the news, and in the people with whom I interact every day. That is a problem which I am dedicated to solving any way I can, with this book serving as my first step towards that goal.

There are many, many people in the world who have been diagnosed with some sort of mental illness, and there are over one million people in the United States alone who have been diagnosed with schizophrenia. Often, the media in its various forms puts a spin on schizophrenics that simply is not true, and I feel that I, and many other people I have met who share this same diagnosis, am living proof of that.

Jim Stallings

I have called myself crazy and written that I have done insane things in this book, but that by no means makes me a threat to myself or anyone else, which is something I feel cannot be stressed enough. Back during my senior year of high school, I remember watching a television program about a SWAT team who had cornered a man in an abandoned house. The man had apparently attacked his girlfriend and then ran to this abandoned house and boarded himself in the attic and was keeping the police at bay with an automatic weapon.

When a SWAT team representative was given camera time to explain the situation, he informed anyone who was watching that the man had been diagnosed with schizophrenia and that he had not been taking his medication. Suddenly, the music became very dramatic, and the SWAT team officer lowered his eyes and shook his head as if to infer that this was indeed a very horrible situation to have this lunatic on the loose who was off of his medication, out of control, and out of his mind.

It is things like this that are all over the media that really gets under my skin. I was with a group of people when I saw this SWAT team special report, and I noticed out of the corner of my eye that a few of the people who were in the room were giving me funny looks and elbowing each other when they thought that I could not see them.

In the case of mental patients, the statistical numbers of us who are not criminals and who have become successful members of our communities are overshadowed by the doubts and fears that allege that we are all dangerous lunatics. These sentiments of doubt and fear go hand in hand with a diagnosis of mental illness, and I for one feel that it is fundamentally not fair.

The feelings that I am outlining, the feelings of fear and discomfort, translate to all walks of life for someone who has been diagnosed with something like schizophrenia. There is a sort of unchecked discrimination that ranges from people treating a mental patient differently, all the way through the legal systems and into the fields of insurance. I, and many other people like myself, will have to pay about three times as much for health insurance coverage as a person who has not been diagnosed with a mental illness, and these increased rates often lead to people not being able to afford the medicine that they may desperately need in order to function successfully.

In my research, I have heard of and spoken to many people who were not able to even get jobs when potential employers found out that that person has been diagnosed with some sort of mental illness. Just the mere fact that an employer knows that a person applying for a job has been in a psychiatric hospital or has been taking some kind of medication to combat their symptoms can sadly keep that person from being hired.

In my own personal history, some people have treated me differently when they have heard about my diagnosis with schizophrenia and that I have been hospitalized for it twice. There were a few people when I was back in high school who would actually walk on the opposite side of the hallway as me when they saw me coming towards them. I have never let this sort of thing bother me or slow me down; rather, I have felt very sorry for people who are so close-minded and fearful, which all helped to give birth to my "Good, f*** 'em" philosophy.

More recently, I knew an individual who became very concerned because I had been spending time with a friend of his. My friend had told this individual briefly that I am a schizophrenic and that I had been in a psychiatric hospital twice, and this young man who had never met me before warned my friend right away that I am dangerous. As soon as he heard very briefly about my past, he went online and did about an hour or so of research and decided that he knew all about me. He told my friend that he was very concerned for her safety, and that it was probably not such a good idea that she was spending so much time alone with me. He even went so far as to ask my friend if she removes sharp objects from the room when I am around.

I am not necessarily blaming this individual for his actions and ignorant beliefs, but I am blaming the media and most of the world at large. There seems to be nothing but doom and gloom stories anywhere you look about people with schizophrenia, and this individual had been caught up in the sentiments that most of the world seems to share. There are not enough stories out there about people like me who have been able to deal with their situation and their diagnosis to create a positive, and extremely safe, outcome.

My most recent doctor, who I mentioned earlier and the person who motivated me to finally write this book, briefly shared my history with one of her colleagues. After a few minutes hearing about my past and current situation, her colleague, who has never even met me, decided that I was in for a disaster. My psychologist informed me that her colleague had told her that he was surprised that I had actually been functioning without medication for so long, and that I was certainly bound to either commit suicide or have a massive relapse and have to be committed to a psychiatric hospital.

This seems to be the sentiment no matter where you go, and this sentiment can very easily trap people into believing that there is no hope other than endless amounts of medication and hospitalization. I have been told by doctors as well as by people who are not involved in the medical community that I am on a path headed for self-destruction, and I for one am getting pretty sick and tired of it.

For me personally, problems arise when people do not take the time to get to know me and only base their opinion on what they have seen in movies or on television. The words delusions, hallucinations, psychotic episodes, and schizophrenia are all very scary words to most people who do not fully understand what they mean, and that is what needs to change. I have also found that most people are scared or afraid to admit that they have a family member or have themselves been diagnosed with some sort of mental illness. It seems that the decades of trying to hide and keep mental illness diagnoses in the dark have in general made most people very afraid of them altogether, and that deeply saddens me.

I have seen many, many times in and out of the psychiatric unit that patients have oftentimes been told to limit who they tell about their experiences, or they have been instructed not to tell people at all. I have seen and heard of family members essentially disowning other patients in light of their mental illnesses or keeping their family member's diagnosis a secret from everyone. I feel that this is a horribly detrimental practice, both for the patient and for everyone else.

The discriminatory practices that are in place today, whether they be conscious actions or not, will never be solved without furthering the knowledge about mental illness and the personal stories of the patients who have been diagnosed. If more and more patients would become comfortable enough to speak openly about themselves to other people, then I feel that everyone would benefit. Patients would no longer live in fear of the negative and scary stigmas that follow after a diagnosis has been made, and people in general would learn and grow a great deal.

It can be a very frustrating thing to have the people around you scared of you or worried about what you might do next, and it is even more frustrating when people you have never met decide that they know what is best for you and consequently pass judgment on you. I have felt that kind of sting many times, and I assure you it is not pleasant, as you can well imagine.

If more people would try and understand fully what it means to be something like a schizophrenic and not just assume right away that all people with this diagnosis are dangerous or complete lunatics, then the world would be a much nicer place for about fifty-one million people. There are many very basic and fundamental thinking processes that need to be revamped in order to obtain this new way of viewing people who have been diagnosed with some sort of mental illness, especially schizophrenia, which is generally considered to be the worst and most destructive of all the mental illnesses that we know of and have catalogued today.

Chapter 10
All in Your Head

Living with paranoid schizophrenia for the last five years has obviously had its impacts on me, both negatively and positively, and I have most certainly learned a lot about myself. I believe that I have successfully come to a solution concerning my schizophrenia and how to deal with it. Instead of running away and being frightened by it and trying to hide it or mask its impact on me by taking different medications, I have embraced it and I have even learned how to enjoy and benefit from it. I believe that I have successfully conquered something that at first seemed impossible to overcome, and I could not be happier with where I am today.

The experiences of our past create and shape the people who we are in the present, and I would never have been the same individual that I am today if it had not been for this amazing chapter of my life. I have seen, or at least experienced in my own little world, some incredible things, both bad and good, and I would not trade these experiences for anything in the world. I now have a solid handle on determining whether or not something is only real to me without the help of medication and psychotherapy, and I am very excited to see where all this takes me in the future.

I do not consider myself an extraordinary individual or a hero of any kind; I am first and foremost a realist. It is not that I have overcome the impossible; obviously it is possible for me to function today as I do. All that I did was that I decided that I needed to gain control of my mind, and I experimented for a long time to figure out the best way to do it. To me, the reality of living with antipsychotic medications flowing through my bloodstream for the rest of my life is not something that I am interested in, so I actively worked to change that reality. I have said before, and I will say again until the day I die, life is all about choices.

Just as a person can choose to work to become successful in anything—a job, a marriage or relationship, academic en-

deavors, or anything else, for that matter—
I chose to become successful at life while
living every day with schizophrenia. It took
a long time to get to where I am today, and
I swore to myself long ago that I will never
let this slow me down, and for the last two
years and counting, I have successfully
kept that promise to myself.

I consider myself very lucky and blessed
in terms of family and friends, and I could
not have progressed as successfully as I
have without their help. I found an incredible amount of strength from my parents,
brothers, and friends when things seemed
all but hopeless, and for that, I owe them
everything. A good support structure and
network of people who support you is absolutely essential to anyone who is attempting to overcome a problem, be it schizophrenia, depression, bipolar disorder, or
anything that presents a roadblock in life,
and anyone who wishes to solve a problem
must realize this and draw strength from
those closest to you. No man or woman is
an island, and believe me when I say that

having something like paranoid schizophrenia will drive that point home in no time at all.

And finally, I consider myself lucky in the fact that I do have schizophrenia and that I now have the chance to share what I have personally gone through with the world. If I can work to change at least one person's view and attitude towards mental patients, I can die a happy man. It is my sincere desire that through this book, I can reach and change the hearts and minds of everyone who reads it and teach people that there is nothing to be afraid of when it comes to mental patients.

I have been through a lot, have experienced some terrible things that I hope to never relive again, been to incredible lows, and have pulled myself out of them to reach even more incredible heights. I have lived life for a number of years on medications that did not allow me to think or experience the world in the manner that I wanted to, and I have lived life without medication and have been very happy ever since. It is true that I experience the world very differently from the "normal"

142

person, and my experience of the world even differs greatly from that of the typical schizophrenic, but I would not change a thing. I am very happy with the person I have become, and I know that I will continue to feel that way for a very long time.

Chapter 11
A Parent's Perspective

THE EARLY YEARS

Jim always seemed different. Not in a bad way, not in a good way, just different. He was our second (of eventually three) boys and we had only been doing the parent thing for 17 months with his older brother when Jim was born so different just meant different than his brother. We figured all kids are different and chalked it up to that.

As I re-read the first paragraph, and try to get started putting down my thoughts, it screams to be further explained. Jim came into this world differently. He was a breach birth and the CAT scan taken of him just before he was born looked like a frog splayed out, upside down and backwards. He was supposed to be head down. He wasn't.

Jim Stallings

He was supposed to be face forward, he wasn't. When his mom and I looked at the film, the doctor said congratulations, you bought yourself a c-section. All his mother and I could think was *it's a frog.*

I got to sit by the side of the operating table as the doctor performed the c-section and brought Jim into the world. The experience was totally different from the birth of our first which was long and drawn-out but ultimately a natural delivery. Jim, on the other hand didn't seem to want to come into this world. He clung to the environment he had come to know over the first 9 months of existence. The doctor tugged multiple times on a bluish gray leg protruding from mom's abdomen. Maybe the incision was too small, maybe Jim just liked things the way they were but the tugging seemed to go on for way too long. As Jim emerged, I kept waiting for the loud cry but it didn't come right away. I narrated the play by play for my wife who was blocked from seeing the action by a drape. "He's blue, he's still blue, he's still blue." It seemed like several minutes went by but I don't think it was that long. The delivery team suctioned his mouth, cut the cord and we heard the first beautiful sound to come from Jim's mouth. He was a beautiful baby. His nose was a bit crooked because it had been jammed up against mom's spinal cord for a while but, other than that, he was really beautiful.

Growing up, Jim always seemed to have lots of friends and was typically at the center of all the activities. I always thought there was something special about Jim but I just didn't know what it was. I supposed all parents think their kids are special in some way but that's not what I mean. It's hard for me to put down on paper what I mean by special but I always thought Jim was.

Maybe it was his unrelenting pursuit of knowledge about wildlife and dinosaurs. Sure, all kids like animals and dinosaurs, but Jim's interest went beyond that. Jim absorbed information about nature, the planet, and animals. We had a multi VHS set entitled "Life on Earth" which Jim watched over and over. He could tell you anything about any animal or life form, existing or extinct. It sort of got to be a joke with his teachers and Cub Scout leaders. "If Jim says anything about animals, you can take it to the bank, don't argue with him because he'll always be right." He seemed to be a walking encyclopedia on the subject.

Maybe it was his creativity. Jim always seemed to look at the world through a more creative and artistic eye than most people. Mom and dad are both business people, trained in the analytic processes and calculating methods of industry. Jim didn't get math, couldn't care less about math, and didn't know the first thing about analytics. He was, and always has been, very gifted when it comes to the arts. He loves to be on stage, to paint or to dazzle people with his ability on the saxophone. Unlike mom and dad, he loves to be in the middle of things, front stage; the spokesperson.

Maybe it was his good looks. Jim has always been handsome; the kid everyone found attractive and appealing. His mom and I always thought Jim was good look-ing. I know all parents think that their kids are the best looking in the crowd; "don't call my baby ugly." I'm sure there is some of that going on with me but Jim is good looking.

Jim has never heard me, or to my knowl-edge, heard his mom reveal this deep dark secret. We joked that because of his good looks, sensitivity to nature, artistic abilities and so on, maybe Jim is gay and that's what's different. We always knew he was different but we just didn't know how he was different. Gay would have been ok. We have lots of family members and friends who are gay. Jim just seemed different.

Maybe it was his chivalrous attitude and behavior. All kids are innocent and pure but Jim has always had a sense of honesty and "knighthood" about him that seemed to fit more in the middle ages than in the 20th century. Jim was named after his uncle who was an Eagle Scout, Air Born Ranger, Green Beret, Special Forces, Colonel in the Army. I always thought his Uncle Jim was

Jim Stallings

born in the wrong era and should have been a Knight in King Arthur's Court. Jim is so much like his uncle. Always it seems, always Jim thinks about others first; at least in the big things in life, not so much in the small things like cleaning his room so mom and dad won't have to but in life's important things.

Maybe it was his other health issues. Jim has always had a plethora of health issues. Way more than his fair share I always thought. From the time he was a baby he has suffered from asthma. We lugged the "breathing treatment machine" around in the car, on airplanes, on vacations and everywhere. We spent our share of time in the emergency room in the middle of the night with an acute asthma attack. I always felt so sorry for Jim having to endure the endless needles, harsh lights of the ER, and breathing treatments. He never complained, he never seemed to resent the fact that he had asthma and none of his friends did. He just didn't like the shots. Later on Jim developed a fairly healthy case of vitiligo, the progressive skin disease that causes patches of skin to lose their pigment and turn white. You would think that such ailments would be devastating to a kid because other kids can be so cruel and ostracizing. Jim always seemed to wear his differences as badges of honor rather than something to hide. Maybe deep inside, these issues troubled him but I was always amazed at how well Jim coped. They didn't seem to be issues to run away from but more like cool things to take into show and tell.

Yes Jim is different and he always has been. To this day I have a hard time putting my finger on why Jim is different but I know that it is a good thing that he is different. I know that because Jim is different he will make an impact on me and others in ways I still don't understand.

ONSET

Jim's early high school years seemed unremarkable. He was involved heavily in the music programs in the Catholic High School he attended. His grades were good but not great. He took Driver's Ed and got his license. He started dating (maybe he isn't gay we thought). Jim always seemed to have a large group of really close friends who surrounded him and supported him. He always dated the most beautiful girls and seemed to be everyone's friend. He had lots of friends who were girls and he had lots of girlfriends. Life was good. Just like Ward and June Cleaver or Ozzie and Harriett Nelson. Our boys were our pride and joy and we couldn't have thought life could be more perfect.

I will never forget the evening Jim came into our bedroom crying and seeming scared, afraid and confused. He jumped into his mom's lap and poured out his heart. He told us freighting stories of hearing voices and seeing people. He didn't understand it but he knew something was wrong. He knew he couldn't deal with it by himself.

These episodes had been happening for months but we never suspected anything. I suppose parents always say that.

How I Lost My Mind and Found Myself

Looking back I always wonder if there wasn't some warning sign or some behavior that we should have latched onto as significant and taken action sooner. Who knows? You can always beat yourself up. Monday morning quarterbacks are always right.

We weren't exactly sure what was happening but we knew it was serious and we needed to get help right away. That is easier said than done. As great as our health care system in the US is, our understanding, even in the medical community, about mental illness is something out of the Dark Ages. We don't understand it, we don't like it, we make fun of it, but most of all, we don't make it easy for those in need to find their way into the healthcare system gracefully and seamlessly as you would if you broke your arm. I was amazed at how difficult it is to enter the medical system seeking help with mental illness. I think it would have been easier to find someone to perform an exorcism than a medical professional who knew how to help.

Jim Stallings

We live in relatively affluent suburbs of a major metropolitan area. The hospital we go to and the health care providers we use are top notch, ranked nationally and represent the epitome of the medical profession. But, call up your pediatrician or primary care provider and explain what is happening and seek advice and referral to medical help and your pleas seem to fall on deaf ears. Not deaf in the sense that they don't hear you or don't have empathy for your situation but deaf in the sense that they seemingly don't have the foggiest notion what they ought to recommend. So, in the middle of this great health care system we were practically relegated to letting our fingers do the walking through the Yellow Pages. Can you imagine? Terrified that something horrible is happening to your child and the medical professionals you have come to rely on, don't seem to have a clue.

There simply isn't a graceful way into the medical system for those with mental illness. After trying for over a week to find the right answer and being rebuffed at each call, we finally took Jim to the psychiatric emergency room at the University of Michigan Hospital. A psychiatrist our family knows there who runs the Psychiatric ER suggested that the only way to "enter" the system given our week-long fiasco of beating our heads against the wall, was to "bring him in."

What a harsh way to get help. Psychiatric Emergency Rooms are not that different from the way they are portrayed in the black and white movies of the 1950's. Locked doors, armed guards, lots of protective glass behind which sit, the medical professionals; it is all very scary, but that was the only way for Jim to enter the system.

Jim was under the legal age of 18 so he was admitted to the children and adolescent psychiatric ward at the University of Michigan Mott's Children's Hospital. He was there for a week the first time he was hospitalized, in a locked and secure psychiatric ward.

Jim Stallings

COMING TO GRIPS

Jim was diagnosed with paranoid schizophrenia and we had the best medical help available. The diagnosis and the reality of what Jim and we were dealing with hit pretty hard. Talk about "didn't see that coming." Stuff like this doesn't happen to June and Ward Clever so how can it be happening to us? How can this be happening to Jim?

As I said earlier, my wife and I are trained in business, both with MBA's and both with significant business experience in the hardball world of public accounting and the auto industry. So, of course, we wanted answers. We wanted to run the numbers and see the actuarial forecasts. What are the odds, what's the prognosis, what's the treatment, when does he get better, how long does this last? Of course, what we found out is that there are no easy answers and nobody, I mean nobody, seems to understand the illness in a way that is satisfactory for the parents of someone who has the problem.

How I Lost My Mind and Found Myself

Jim was hospitalized twice during his high school years. His mother and I tried to understand what he was going through but, frankly, we didn't do a very good job. Of course he was being seen by the best psychiatrists at the University of Michigan and, of course, we were in the family support groups which met once a week. Jim kept trying to explain what was happening to him but, to this day, I can't say I really understand it. When we got to the point where we understood the symptoms and could openly talk to Jim about them, I still had a very difficult time truly understanding the pain Jim lived on a daily basis. Jim would tell me that his delusions are as real as I was. "It is just like someone telling me that you're not here in the room talking to me; I wouldn't believe them." Jim would say. I didn't get it. As hard as I tried, I couldn't understand. What I have come to understand is that schizophrenia is a frightening illness and those who deal with its ravages on a daily basis are strong beyond what those of us without the illness can possibly comprehend.

Jim Stallings

I suppose the hardest thing about coming to grips with the illness as a parent is the uncertainty. Jim's psychiatrist actually told me that a third of the people with the illness get worse, a third get better, and a third stay the same. What hope is that? I think there is sort of a "truth in lending" unspoken law in the medical profession that is brought about by the vast number of malpractice lawsuits in this country. The doctors are so hesitant to hold out any hope because they might be wrong and then they have legal liability somehow.

I think the scariest thing I heard during this period of time was that there is a strong likelihood that Jim will not be able to function adequately in the adult world and will need care the rest of his life.

It seemed like there was an endless stream of pills, psychiatrist visits, and balancing the medications and declining function. The more medications Jim took, the less he was able to function. Somehow the doctors didn't seem to understand that the cure was worse than the disorder. I fail to understand to this day how medicating someone to near the point of unconsciousness is a treatment. "High five's all around; Jim's symptoms are improving. He barely hears voices anymore and Douglas hasn't been around in a while. Great." However, he sleeps about 20 hours a day, has trouble dressing himself in the morning and his grades went from pretty good to "oh crap."

During this whole ordeal, Jim was remarkable. He never wanted to hide his disorder from anyone or run away from it. Sure some of his friends ran for cover but others, his real friends, stood by him in a way that defines what friendship really is. There was, and continues to be, a bit of a rift between me and my wife about how to handle the situation with the outside world. Do we tell people or try and sweep it under the rug. I've always been of the opinion that "it is what it is" and that you need to step up to the challenges. If people don't like the fact that you have paranoid schizophrenia, then that's tough. I learned a lot from Jim as he was trying to cope with what he was going through. He always hit it head on. He told me once that "if my friends can't deal with me this way then maybe they aren't really my friends." What a way to look at the world.

I think the thing that amazed me most about Jim during this time was his willingness to talk about what he was going through. He sought out opportunities to speak in front of his high school class and talked about his symptoms and the onset of the disorder. He told me that when his symptoms first started he had no idea what was going on and that maybe his speaking to high school students might make it easier for someone else coming down with the symptoms. He also thought that he could have an impact on the friends of those with schizophrenia or any other mental illness. His friends meant so much to him and I think he wanted to share that with others who might one day find themselves with a friend who might be suffering.

Jim's grades declined and then slipped further. This was all happening during the later phases of his junior year; prime college application time. He was barely able to dress himself much less devise and execute a plan to apply to colleges.

Then a remarkable thing happened. Something that was totally unexpected but very welcomed. Jim seemed to be getting better. He was less groggy and "drugged up" and more able to function. Maybe the doctors have finally hit on the right combination of drugs to relieve the symptoms but not render Jim unconscious most of the time. Could it be? I wanted to believe it so much. I wanted to think that Jim was the exception, one of the people who will get better and maybe beat this thing. Almost symptom free, back to "normal." Life was good again.

Jim is strong willed and very determined. He decided that even if the doctors "knew better" about what was good for him, that it was better to live with the symptoms and be part of the world than it was to live life in a semi-conscious state, sleeping most of the day but be relatively

Jim Stallings

free from symptoms. So, the only thing to do was to pretend to take the meds, and pretend there were no symptoms. That's exactly what Jim did.

For a while I let myself believe that there were no symptoms and the medication really works; we just needed to find the right dosages and the right combinations. I admit that after a while, I had my suspicions that things were not as advertised but I didn't want to believe it was back.

My wife and I were confronted by Jim and his girlfriend about the cover-up. We heard tales of dangerous behavior that put both Jim and others at risk because of the delusions and voices. We knew he was going to be hospitalized again.

Jim did get through high school and graduate. He won the John Phillip Souza award for the best senior musician in his school. He was elected to the Band Counsel. He was the only senior in the history of the school to put on a "senior recital" where he played his saxophone with other

162

peers on stage at the school followed by a reception at our house. With a little help from dad, he applied to and got into a Big 10 School. He turned 18 and became an adult so mom and dad no longer hold sway over directing medical treatment and the goings and comings of a young man.

Jim is resolutely opposed to taking the medications prescribed by his doctors. He is determined that through sheer will power and strength of character, he can overcome his illness. He can learn to ignore the voices and delusions.

When Jim entered Michigan State we met with the resident psychiatrist at the campus health clinic. She advised strongly that Jim needed to be on his medications and that the likelihood of him making it through college without the medication was very low. Jim listened politely and said no rather impolitely-I think he should have just called and cancelled his appointments and not just showed up.

Jim Stallings

Jim became more and more interested in helping others understand the disorder he lives with every day. He continues to speak to high schools, university classes and has now, added med students to the groups to whom he speaks.

He wanted so much to share his experiences with others and to help those who would listen that he wrote this book. He asked me to help him through the process of writing and publishing a book, something I knew nothing about, so I did some research and asked some friends who have been published.

Jim wrote the manuscript and formed a little company, Eden Roc Publishing, LLC to publish it. Did I mention how proud I am?

I'm worried about him, but whatever happens, I know that someone, somewhere will be better off because of what Jim has done to educate people about his illness. Life's a journey. Enjoy it, whatever it brings.

Chapter 12
Mom's Chapter

Earlier....

Jim came into the world upside down and backwards. People I worked with during my first two pregnancies kept telling me the second baby, Jim, had to be a girl because I was carrying him so differently. But, rather than female, he was breech. After the CAT scan was completed to determine in what position he was, the doctor and techs giggled behind the screen. They asked me to crawl off the table and take a look. All I could say was, "Good God, I'm giving birth to a frog." When Jim was old enough for sarcasm we used to tell him that he was a non-conformist from the start and had assumed a "froggal" position en utero just to be different.

From the beginning, he was beautiful—crooked nose and all. He was an early walker—first steps on the day he turned eight months—and an early talker—full sentences by age 24 months. He loved animals, nature, and dinosaurs and very early on in pre-school was correcting teachers who learned not to question his wisdom in certain areas.

During grade school, Jim was popular. He learned to play the sax, won awards for art and was a good student. He wasn't perfect—kept a messy room, didn't get A's in math—but he wasn't a behavior problem. Since the "gay gene" seems to run in my family, Jim's strong interest in art had us jokingly wondering. He did have chronic asthma that kept him tied to a machine for years and, the over achiever that he was, he developed a great case of vitiligo at an earlier than normal age.

During High School, Jim had very nice, beautiful girlfriends, and he continued to be popular. His grades were good. He was in the band and also greatly involved with the track and field team. What I am trying to say is, as far as we knew, Jim was "normal," he was an achiever, he had friends, he was handsome, he was the heart throb of the girls' school, he was artistic, he was funny. We did not have a clue as to what was to come.

But, oh My God…..

The nightmare started when one spring evening during his junior year of high school. Jim, his father, and I had an argument that night and later he described the voices he was hearing, the visits from Douglas and how he saw people on the roof of his school. His father and I sat there and listened, dumbfounded, not knowing what to say. Jim left our room and, after a few minutes, came back with a box of knives that he had been keeping in his room for protection and stormed out more frightened than I had ever seen him before. I looked at my husband and said, "You're the psych major, but this sounds like schizophrenia to me!"

It Begins….

Jim Stallings

The one thing his father and I did not do was to go into denial and recognized that this was serious. We had no inkling of it before, but the way Jim confronted us made us realize that this was real and he wanted help. If any parents reading this take anything from this book, it would be to skip the denial phase, skip the phone phase and check your child into the closest and best emergency psychiatric facility you can find.

Just as Rick, Jim's father, said, it was almost two weeks of endless phone calls trying to get someone, anyone, to take Jim on as a patient. This doctor did not treat children, that doctor did not treat people with these types of symptoms...but they all knew someone else who did. Just give that doctor a call. We finally ended up taking him to Psychiatric Emergency to get him into the system. What that means is: you hand your child, your beautiful baby, over to a lock down facility where he must surrender his belt, shoestrings, or anything that can be used to hurt himself or another patient. Your visitation is very limited. All I could think of was "One Flew Over the Cuckoo's Nest".

While his father and I felt guilty for putting Jim in such a place, questioned whether we had over reacted, whether we had "marked" him for life, etc., etc., etc., Jim showed the courage that was going to be the hallmark of how he was to face this disorder. The University of Michigan Hospital and its staff were wonderful. Jim soon became a favorite. Jim had us bring his sax which had to be locked up and he played for the staff and other patients. One small boy who had not spoken in a long time, listened to Jim play and said, "I play the trumpet." His parents couldn't get home and back fast enough with his trumpet. He and Jim played together. We do not know what has happened to that little boy, but we do know that Jim had a profound effect on him.

The next two years were spent trying to get Jim adjusted to his medications, attending family support groups, and working with his psychiatrist to determine what

Jim's prognosis was. During this time, Jim alternated between being a zombie and delusions. I remember crying on the phone with his doctor saying, "We're losing him, he can't function on these drugs and he is still seeing Douglas." Only to be reassured that the high functioning, intelligent victims of schizophrenia, such as Jim, usually commit suicide. It was a parent's nightmare.

Do not think that we just sat around dealing with Jim's problems or that Jim just sat there. In spite of this devastating diagnosis, life went on. During this time, we opened two new businesses. Jim graduated from High School earning the highest award in music given by his school and the Coach's Award for Track & Field. He applied—with a lot of help from his father—to college and was accepted to Michigan State. However, at other times, he would race into the house, out of breath, scared out of his mind asking if there was really a white van across the street. Of course there wasn't, but it took a lot of reassuring and often going across the street and "walking through" the van to convince him. We spent a lot of time on the phone with his psychiatrist asking how to deal with each new development.

I was of the opinion that Jim's disorder should only be revealed on a "need to know basis." I was raised that what happened in the family stayed in the family. I was also concerned that Jim would be ostracized because schizophrenia is considered by many to be very frightening. Jim was of the opinion that it is what it is and that there was no reason to hide it. I was wrong. People were very supportive. His girlfriend accompanied Jim and, usually, his father to the support group meetings. His friends were still his friends and only a few treated him differently. His teachers did what they could to help him. He has also talked to psychology and psychiatry students at University of Michigan, Purdue and local high schools to give them, as he said, "a human face to a very scary disorder."

It continues...

Jim Stallings

The most difficult part of trying to support someone with this disorder is to not treat him or her with kid gloves. Jim does not want to be treated differently but it is hard to know when too much is too much. Do I, as a parent, make the same demands of him as my other children? I am very proud of Jim. How he has faced his problems and his desire to help others facing schizophrenia is truly inspirational.

Chapter 13
John's Chapter, How He Lost His Mind and I Found Mine

There are few occurrences in a person's life as drastic as what Jim went through. All around him were new experiences and changes in perception that before now he had never thought possible. While this was going on, a young boy who aged only eleven was oblivious to his surroundings. He was still wrapped up in his grade school world where he was not concerned with anyone but himself.

One night it all changed, and this eleven year old boy has said this night to be one of the many defining moments of his development into a person, and one of the defining moments of his life. The hardest thing for him to understand was that the events that took place were not his events to be a part of—he was only a spectator. How could all of this impact his life on such a grand scale, when he barely understood even the simplest of things in the world around him?

That night, as this certain boy was simply watching television, he heard a commotion in the kitchen of his house. His next door neighbor and girlfriend to his brother walked into the room, and spoke a few words to his mother. Still only watching, he had no idea what was going on. As any inquisitive child does, he asked what was going on. His mother replied that they were going to take his brother to the hospital. He was hearing voices and seeing people, and these voices and people were not really there.

The boy walked down to the garage where his brother, dad, and brother's girlfriend were getting into the car to go to the hospital. Tears were streaming down his face, but as he looks back upon these events he does not know why the tears were there. His mother turned to him and told him to stop, at least until the car pulled away. When the head lights were no longer visible, his mother started crying and embraced the young boy, but the boy was not crying as he had before. His conscience was eating at him and telling him to be upset and to let out a few tears, but he could not do it.

That took place five years ago, and as the boy is now more grown up, he realizes now why he couldn't cry when the event called for tears. His brother, the bravest person he knows, was going for help; help with a burden he had carried for eight months alone by himself, and that was nothing to cry over. That single act of bravery is the definition of a hero. The boy's brother did not pull him from a burning car or anything of that nature; he did more for the boy than he will ever know. Now, at the age of sixteen, that same boy from five years ago still has only one image when the word hero is mentioned: his brother Jim

Jim is my brother and he does, in fact, have paranoid schizophrenia. Countless people have asked me, often times with fearful looks on their faces, about my brother and how he is doing. I simply reply that he is better than okay: he has grown stronger than most people in the world. Sure three hospitalizations and antipsychotic medications is something scary to the world, but not to me. My brother has become one of the greatest sources of inspiration for me in my life, and although my problems may not match up in comparison to the things that he has been through, his bravery and his ability to become a better person through hard times can be applied to all hardships I, or anyone for that matter, face.

One of the greatest experiences of my life was talking to my brother until the early hours of the morning about everything he had been through. The reality of the false images his brain portrays to him is shocking. The words I remember most from that long talk were this:

"You and I could both be fake right now; for all you know, you could be an eighty year old woman in a coma whose brain is just making up this false life. The person I talked to for twenty minutes in the hallway could not have been real. We do not know who we are or why we have been given the lives we have been given, but to hell with it, you're doing a pretty stand up job even if you are just an eighty year old woman in a coma." You can tell that his sense of humor was never affected by the things he's been through.

All of that is true. We do not know who we are or why we are. But my brother has taught me perhaps the greatest lesson I have ever learned: if I get knocked down, I will get up taller than before, and faster, and be better because of it. Any bad situation can make you a good, no a great person. Through my brother's courage and through his extraordinary actions at such a young age, he may claim that he lost his mind, but in losing his mind he found himself, and gave me, although he may not realize it, something even greater: a hero, a lesson, and something I can use for the rest of my life to make myself a greater person.

"Pain is God's grace, given to those who possess the Courage to bear it."

CPSIA information can be obtained at www.ICGtesting.com
Printed in the USA
BVOW11s2354120515

400127BV00023B/212/P